Advanced Machine Learning Techniques: Theory and Practice

By Khairullah. Khan

Table of Contents

Introduction

In the age of information and technology, the field of machine learning stands at the forefront of a remarkable transformation. Machine learning, a subset of artificial intelligence, has surged in significance, reshaping the way we interact with technology, process data, and make decisions. From self-driving cars and virtual assistants to personalized content recommendations and fraud detection systems, machine learning has seamlessly woven itself into the fabric of our daily lives.

The rapid progress of machine learning is a testament to human ingenuity and innovation. In a span of a few years, we have witnessed remarkable breakthroughs, pushing the boundaries of what machines can achieve. These breakthroughs, enabled by both foundational research and applied engineering, have given birth to a myriad of state-of-the-art techniques and methodologies.

This book, "Advanced Machine Learning Techniques: Theory and Practice," serves as a guided journey through the vibrant landscape of contemporary machine learning. Our objective is clear: to provide you, the reader, with a comprehensive understanding of the cutting edge techniques and technologies that have revolutionized the field. While our focus is on the techniques available up to September 2021, we aim to offer a solid foundation upon which you can build and explore the ever evolving realm of machine learning.

Why is staying abreast of state-of-the-art techniques so essential? The answer lies in the inexorable progress of technology. The machine learning field, much like a living organism, continues to evolve, adapt, and expand its horizons. Methods that were considered groundbreaking just a few years ago may now be standard practice, and new approaches emerge to tackle increasingly complex problems. This book is your key to unlocking the potential of these innovations and understanding how they can be applied to your specific domain.

In the chapters that follow, we will dive deep into a plethora of machine learning techniques and methodologies, from the venerable to the avant-garde. We will explore neural networks, transfer learning, reinforcement learning, generative adversarial networks (GANs), and many more. We will examine their core principles, practical applications, and the impact they have on fields as diverse as healthcare, finance, natural language processing, and quantum computing.

But this book is not merely a technical manual. It's a journey into the world of machine learning that goes beyond the algorithms and models. We will also explore the ethical considerations, the need for fairness, and the ever pressing question of interpretability in machine learning. We'll discuss how these cutting edge technologies impact society, and how we can harness their power responsibly.

The field of machine learning is not just about the equations and code; it's about creativity, innovation, and collaboration. It's about pushing the boundaries of what's possible, and it's about making the world a better place. Our journey begins here, and we invite you to embark with us on this exciting expedition through the realm of "Advances in Machine Learning: Techniques and Applications." Together, we'll unravel the mysteries of this transformative field and discover how to harness its power to shape a brighter future. Let's begin the journey.

Preface:

Welcome to "Advanced Machine Learning Techniques: Theory and Practice." This book represents a comprehensive exploration of the ever evolving world of machine learning, a landscape filled with innovation, promise, and endless possibilities.

Machine learning, a subfield of artificial intelligence, has been on a remarkable journey of discovery and transformation. From the early days of rule based expert systems to the sophisticated neural networks and deep learning models of today, the progression is nothing short of astonishing. The journey has been marked by continuous advancements and paradigm shifting breakthroughs that have redefined the boundaries of what is achievable.

As the authors of this book, we are passionate about the field of machine learning. We have witnessed firsthand the profound impact it has on industries, society, and everyday life. Our collective experience in academia and industry has allowed us to observe the rapid evolution of the field, where novel ideas and approaches emerge at a remarkable pace. It is this vibrant dynamism that has inspired us to create a guide to help you navigate the world of cutting edge machine learning techniques.

Our aim is to provide a valuable resource for both newcomers and seasoned practitioners in the field. We've designed this book to be accessible to those who are just beginning their journey into the world of machine learning, while still offering insights and indepth knowledge for experienced professionals. Our goal is to empower you with the knowledge and tools needed to understand, apply, and adapt the state-of-the-art techniques discussed in these pages.

"Advanced Machine Learning Techniques: Theory and Practice" is organized to be both informative and practical. Each chapter delves into a specific machine learning technique, offering explanations of the underlying concepts, real world applications, and guidance on how to implement these techniques effectively. You will discover the power of deep learning, the versatility of transfer learning, the complexities of reinforcement learning, and the creative capabilities of generative adversarial networks. We also explore emerging areas such as quantum machine learning, self supervised learning, and ethical considerations in AI.

As you read through these pages, you will find not only technical insights but also a deep appreciation for the ethical and social implications of machine learning. In an era where machine learning increasingly shapes our lives, we emphasize the importance of responsible and ethical use of this technology. This book aims to foster a holistic understanding of machine learning, encompassing not only the "how" but also the "why" and the "what if."

The journey through these pages represents the culmination of our collective experiences and the knowledge we've gained over the years. We are thrilled to share our insights with you and hope that this book serves as a valuable resource on your own journey into the captivating world of machine learning.

We invite you to embark on this adventure with us, exploring the techniques, applications, and ethical considerations that make machine learning a field of boundless opportunities and limitless horizons. As you read through the chapters, engage with the practical examples, and ponder the ethical implications, we encourage you to think not just about the technology itself, but the profound ways in which it can change the world for the better.

Machine learning has the potential to shape the future in ways we can only begin to imagine. We hope that "Advances in Machine Learning: Techniques and Applications" empowers you to be a part of that exciting journey.

Happy reading, learning, and innovating.

Prof. Dr. Khairullah Khan

The Authors

Acknowledgments

Writing a book is a collaborative effort that involves the support and contributions of many individuals and organizations. We would like to express our deep appreciation for everyone who has been a part of this journey, directly or indirectly, and has made this book possible.

First and foremost, we extend our gratitude to the dedicated team at my colleagues Mr. Qureshi Khan and Mian Shaukat who believed in the vision of this book and worked tirelessly to bring it to life. Their guidance, expertise, and commitment have been invaluable throughout the writing and publication process.

We also want to thank our colleagues and peers in the field of machine learning who have been constant sources of inspiration and knowledge. The collaborative and ever evolving nature of this field has pushed us to strive for excellence and stay updated with the latest advancements.

Our heartfelt thanks go to the countless researchers, educators, and practitioners who have contributed to the field of machine learning through their work, publications, and open source contributions. Your dedication to advancing the state of the art in this field has been instrumental in shaping the content of this book.

We are also grateful for the support of our families and friends who have stood by us throughout this demanding endeavor. Your encouragement and understanding have been our motivation when the path seemed challenging.

Finally, we express our deepest appreciation to you, the reader. This book was written with the hope of sharing knowledge, sparking curiosity, and fostering a deeper understanding of machine learning. Your interest in the subject matter and your commitment to learning are the driving forces behind our work.

In writing this acknowledgment, we realize that it is impossible to individually name everyone who has played a part in this project. Nevertheless, please know that your contributions, whether direct or indirect, have been significant and deeply appreciated.

This book is dedicated to all those who seek to push the boundaries of knowledge, harness the power of machine learning, and make a positive impact on the world. Thank you for joining us on this exciting journey.

With heartfelt appreciation,

Porf. Dr. Khairullah Khan

13/10/2023

Chapter 1: Deep Learning Theory and Practice

1.1   Introduction

Deep learning is at the forefront of the machine learning revolution, propelling our ability to solve complex problems and process vast amounts of data. In this chapter, we embark on a journey into the realm of deep learning, beginning with the fundamental building blocks: neural networks.

Deep learning is a rapidly evolving field of artificial intelligence with the potential to revolutionize many industries. By understanding the basic concepts of deep learning theory, we can better understand how deep learning models work and how they can be used to solve real-world problems.

Deep learning is a type of machine learning that uses artificial neural networks to learn from data. Neural networks are inspired by the structure and function of the human brain, and they are made up of interconnected nodes, called neurons, which process information and pass it on to other neurons.

Deep learning models are trained on large datasets of examples, and they learn to identify patterns in the data and make predictions based on those patterns. This makes deep learning models well-suited for a wide variety of tasks, including image recognition, natural language processing, and machine translation.

One of the key advantages of deep learning is its ability to learn from data. Deep learning models do not need to be explicitly programmed to perform a task. Instead, they can be trained on a dataset of examples, and they will learn to perform the task by identifying patterns in the data. This makes deep learning models well-suited for tasks that would be difficult or impossible to program explicitly.

Another advantage of deep learning is its ability to generalize to new data. Deep learning models do not over fit the training data, meaning that they can generalize to new data that they have never seen before. This makes deep learning models well-suited for real-world applications, where the data is often noisy and variable.

Deep learning theory is a complex and rapidly evolving field, but there are a few key concepts that are important to understand:

- Artificial neural networks: Artificial neural networks are the building blocks of deep learning models. Neural networks are made up of interconnected nodes, called neurons, which process information and pass it on to other neurons.

- Representation learning: Representation learning is the process of learning to represent data in a way that is useful for the task at hand. Deep learning models learn to represent data by extracting features from the data at multiple levels of abstraction.

- Back propagation: Back propagation is an algorithm that is used to train deep learning models. Back propagation works by calculating the error of the model's predictions and then propagating that error back through the network, adjusting the weights of the neurons as it goes.

1.2 Neural Networks and Their Evolution

Neural networks are a type of machine learning algorithm that are inspired by the structure and function of the human brain. They are made up of interconnected nodes, called neurons, which process information and pass it on to other neurons. Neural networks can be trained to perform a wide variety of tasks, including image recognition, natural language processing, and machine translation.

Neural networks were first proposed in the 1950s, but they did not become widely used until the late 2000s, when advances in computing power and data availability made it possible to train large and complex neural networks. This led to a revolution in the field of artificial intelligence, with neural networks achieving state-of-the-art results on many challenging tasks.

One of the key advantages of neural networks is their ability to learn from data. Neural networks can be trained on large datasets of examples, and they will learn to identify patterns in the data and make predictions based on those patterns. This makes neural networks well-suited for a wide variety of tasks, including tasks that would be difficult or impossible to program explicitly.

Another advantage of neural networks is their robustness to noise and variation in the data. Neural networks do not over-fit the training data, meaning that they can generalize to new data that they have never seen before. This makes neural networks well-suited for real-world applications, where the data is often noisy and variable.

The evolution of neural networks has been driven by a number of factors, including advances in computing power, data availability, and algorithmic research. In the early days of neural networks, training a large neural network could take weeks or even months. However, with the advent of GPUs and other specialized hardware, it is now possible to train large neural networks in a matter of days or hours.

The availability of large datasets has also been a key factor in the evolution of neural networks. Neural networks need large amounts of data to train effectively, and the availability of large datasets from a variety of domains, such as images, text, and audio, has made it possible to train neural networks that can perform a wide range of tasks.

Finally, algorithmic research has also played a key role in the evolution of neural networks. Researchers have developed new algorithms for training neural networks more efficiently and effectively. For example, the development of the back propagation algorithm in the 1970s made it possible to train neural networks with multiple hidden layers. This was a major breakthrough, as it allowed neural networks to learn more complex patterns in the data.

Neural networks are now used in a wide variety of applications, including:

- Image recognition: Neural networks are used to recognize objects and faces in images. This technology is used in a variety of applications, such as self-driving cars, security systems, and social media.

- Natural language processing: Neural networks are used to understand and generate human language. This technology is used in a variety of applications, such as machine translation, chatbots, and voice assistants.

- Machine translation: Neural networks are used to translate text from one language to another. This technology is used in a variety of applications, such as translation tools, social media platforms, and e-commerce websites.

- Medical diagnosis: Neural networks are used to diagnose diseases and recommend treatments. This technology is still in its early stages of development, but it has the potential to revolutionize the field of medicine.

Neural networks are a powerful tool that can be used to solve a wide variety of problems. With the continued advances in computing power, data availability, and algorithmic research, neural networks are likely to become even more powerful and versatile in the future.

1.2.1 The Biological Inspiration

The inspiration for neural networks, a cornerstone of deep learning, is deeply rooted in our quest to understand the human brain. It is not by chance that the term "neural" is used to describe these computational systems. The human brain, with its billions of interconnected neurons, is a marvel of natural engineering, capable of complex tasks ranging from image recognition to natural language understanding.

The idea behind artificial neural networks is to replicate, to some extent, the information processing capabilities of the brain. Just as our brain's neurons are connected through synapses, artificial neural networks consist of interconnected nodes that communicate and process information. These nodes, or "neurons," are the basic units of computation in neural networks. Much like biological neurons, they can receive, process, and transmit information.

1.2.2 Early Beginnings

The roots of neural networks in artificial intelligence date back to the mid20th century. In 1943, Warren McCulloch and Walter Pitts introduced the first mathematical model of a neuron, which laid the foundation for artificial neural networks. Their model simplified the complex mechanisms of a biological neuron into a binary, on/off switch. This binary abstraction allowed for mathematical manipulation, setting the stage for computational models of neurons.

During the same period, the concept of perceptrons emerged, introduced by Frank Rosenblatt in 1957. Perceptrons are single layer neural networks capable of binary classification tasks. They marked a significant step forward in neural network research and were, in many ways, the predecessors of the multilayer neural networks we know today.

1.2.3 The AI Winter and Resurgence

Despite the early promise of neural networks, the field of artificial intelligence entered what became known as the "AI Winter" during the 1970s and 1980s. Progress slowed, and many researchers shifted their focus to other AI approaches. It seemed that the computational power and data required to train complex neural networks were beyond reach at the time.

However, the AI Winter eventually gave way to a new era with the emergence of more powerful hardware, larger datasets, and novel training algorithms. The 1990s and early 2000s witnessed a resurgence of interest in neural networks. Researchers explored multilayer networks, called multilayer perceptrons, and began to develop more effective training methods.

The turning point came with the introduction of the back propagation algorithm, which allowed for efficient training of deep neural networks by propagating errors backward through the network. The combination of larger datasets, faster computers, and improved training techniques reignited interest in deep learning. This resurgence, along with advances in graphical processing units (GPUs) that accelerated neural network training, laid the foundation for the deep learning renaissance.

In the upcoming sections of this chapter, we will delve deeper into the architecture and functioning of neural networks, the role of activation functions, and the practical applications of deep learning. This will provide you with a strong foundation for understanding and working with this powerful machine learning technique.

1.3 Variants of Neural Networks

Neural networks are a type of machine learning algorithm that are inspired by the structure and function of the human brain. They are made up of interconnected nodes, called neurons, which process information and pass it on to other neurons. Neural networks can be trained to perform a wide variety of tasks, including image recognition, natural language processing, and machine translation.

There are many different variants of neural networks, each designed for specific tasks and applications. Some of the most common variants of neural networks include:

- Feed forward neural networks: Feed forward neural networks are the simplest type of neural network. They are made up of a series of layers, with each layer connected to the next. The input data is fed into the first layer, and the output of the network is produced by the last layer. Feed forward neural networks are often used for classification and regression tasks.

- Convolutional neural networks (CNNs): CNNs are a type of feed forward neural network that are designed for image recognition tasks. CNNs use a special type of layer called a convolutional layer to extract features from images. CNNs have been shown to be very effective for a variety of image recognition tasks, including image classification, object detection, and image segmentation.

- Recurrent neural networks (RNNs): RNNs are a type of neural network that are designed to process sequential data, such as text and audio. RNNs have a feedback loop that allows them to learn long-term dependencies in the data. RNNs are often used for natural language processing tasks, such as machine translation and text generation.

- Long short-term memory (LSTM) networks: LSTM networks are a type of RNN that are designed to learn long-term dependencies in the data. LSTM networks have a special type of gate that allows them to control the flow of information through the network. LSTM networks are often used for natural language processing tasks, such as machine translation and text generation.

- Transformer networks: Transformer networks are a type of neural network that are designed for natural language processing tasks. Transformer networks use a self-attention mechanism that allows them to learn long-range dependencies in the data. Transformer networks have been shown to achieve state-of-the-art results on many natural language processing tasks, such as machine translation and text summarization.

These are just a few of the many different variants of neural networks. There are many other variants that have been developed for specific tasks and applications.

Neural networks are a powerful tool that can be used to solve a wide variety of problems. However, it is important to note that neural networks can be complex and expensive to train. Additionally, neural networks can be biased, reflecting the biases in the data that they are trained on.

1.3.1 Convolutional Neural Networks (CNNs)

Convolutional Neural Networks, or CNNs, represent a pivotal breakthrough in deep learning. These specialized neural networks are tailored for tasks involving grid like data, such as images and videos. In this section, we will explore the architecture, workings, and significance of CNNs.

Convolutional neural networks (CNNs) are a type of artificial neural network that are particularly well-suited for image recognition and other tasks that involve processing spatial data. CNNs are inspired by the structure and function of the human visual cortex, and they use a series of convolutional and pooling layers to extract features from images.

One of the key advantages of CNNs is their ability to learn from data. CNNs do not need to be explicitly programmed to identify different features in an image. Instead, they can be trained on a dataset of images, and they will learn to identify features by extracting patterns from the data.

Another advantage of CNNs is their ability to generalize to new data. CNNs do not overfit the training data, meaning that they can identify features in new images that they have never seen before. This makes CNNs well-suited for real-world applications, where the data is often noisy and variable.

CNNs are used in a wide variety of applications, including:

- Image classification: CNNs are used to classify images into different categories, such as cats, dogs, cars, and airplanes.

- Object detection: CNNs are used to detect objects in images, such as people, animals, and vehicles.

- Image segmentation: CNNs are used to segment images into different regions, such as the foreground and background.

- Natural language processing: CNNs are used to process natural language text, such as machine translation and text summarization.

Here is an example of how a CNN might be used to classify an image of a cat:

1. The image is first passed through a series of convolutional layers. Each convolutional layer applies a different set of filters to the image data.

2. The output of the convolutional layers is then passed through a series of pooling layers. The pooling layers reduce the dimensionality of the data while preserving the most important information.

3. The output of the pooling layers is then passed through a few fully connected layers. The fully connected layers make a prediction about the class of the image (e.g., cat, dog, car, etc.).

CNNs have been shown to achieve state-of-the-art results on many challenging image recognition tasks. For example, CNNs are used in self-driving cars to identify objects on the road, and they are used in facial recognition systems to identify people in images.

In addition to the applications listed above, CNNs are also being used for tasks such as medical diagnosis, video analysis, and fraud detection. As CNNs continue to develop and improve, they are likely to be used in even more applications in the future.

The Need for CNNs

Neural networks, while powerful, have limitations when it comes to processing grid data. In tasks like image recognition, where pixel values are spatially correlated, standard neural networks fall short in capturing these patterns effectively. CNNs were designed to address this issue.

The innovation of CNNs lies in their ability to learn hierarchical representations of data. Instead of directly connecting each neuron to every pixel in an image, CNNs employ convolutional layers. These layers are equipped with small filters (kernels) that slide over the input data, extracting local patterns and features. These features are then combined and refined in subsequent layers, allowing CNNs to learn intricate hierarchies of information. This hierarchical learning is one of the key strengths of CNNs and is instrumental in their success in image related tasks.

Architecture of CNNs

CNNs are composed of several types of layers, each serving a specific function. The primary layers include:

Convolutional Layers:

These layers apply convolution operations with learnable filters to the input data. The filters capture various features like edges, textures, or more complex patterns in the data.

Pooling Layers:

Pooling-layers reduce the spatial dimensions of the data by sub-sampling. Common pooling methods include max pooling and average pooling.

Fully Connected Layers:

After several convolutional and pooling layers, CNNs typically end with one or more fully connected layers that perform classification or regression tasks.

Convolution Operation

The core of a CNN is the convolution operation. It involves sliding a filter over the input data, elementwise multiplying the filter values with the corresponding input values, and then summing the results. This process generates feature maps that highlight local patterns in the data. Convolution operations are characterized by hyper parameters like the filter size, the stride (how much the filter moves each step), and the padding (whether to add zeropadding to the input).

CNNs excel in hierarchical feature extraction. In the initial layers, filters capture basic features like edges and corners. As we move deeper into the network, the receptive fields of the filters increase, allowing them to identify more complex features and object parts. This hierarchical representation is crucial for recognizing and classifying complex objects in images.

1.3.2 Recurrent Neural Networks (RNNs)

Recurrent neural networks (RNNs) are a type of artificial neural network that are designed to process sequential data, such as text and audio. RNNs have a feedback loop that allows them to learn long-term dependencies in the data. This makes RNNs well-suited for tasks such as machine translation, text generation, and speech recognition.

Recurrent Neural Networks, or RNNs, represent a class of neural networks designed to work with sequential data. Unlike feed forward neural networks, RNNs have an inherent ability to process data with temporal dependencies, making them invaluable in natural language processing, time series analysis, and various sequential data tasks.

RNNs are typically made up of a series of interconnected layers. Each layer is connected to the previous layer, and to itself. This feedback loop allows RNNs to learn long-term dependencies in the data. For example, an RNN that is trained to translate text from English to French will learn that the English word "I" can be translated to the French word "je" only if the previous word is "I".

RNNs are trained using a variety of algorithms, including back-propagation through time (BPTT). BPTT is a complex algorithm, but it is the most effective way to train RNNs.

RNNs are used in a wide variety of applications, including:

- Machine translation: RNNs are used to translate text from one language to another. RNNs have been shown to achieve state-of-the-art results on many machine translation tasks.

- Text generation: RNNs are used to generate text, such as news articles, blog posts, and creative writing. RNNs have been used to create AI-powered chatbots and writing assistants.

- Speech recognition: RNNs are used to recognize speech. RNNs are used in voice assistants, such as Siri and Alexa, and in speech-to-text applications.

- Music generation: RNNs are used to generate music, such as melodies and rhythms. RNNs have been used to create AI-powered music composers and arrangers.

RNNs are a powerful tool for processing sequential data. RNNs have been used to achieve state-of-the-art results on many challenging tasks, and they are being used in a wide variety of applications.

Challenges of RNNs

One of the main challenges of RNNs is that they can be difficult to train. This is because of the vanishing gradient problem. The vanishing gradient problem occurs when the gradients of the loss function become very small, making it difficult to train the network.

Another challenge of RNNs is that they can be slow to train. This is because RNNs need to process the entire sequence of data at once in order to make a prediction.

Conclusion

RNNs are a powerful tool for processing sequential data. RNNs have been used to achieve state-of-the-art results on many challenging tasks, and they are being used in a wide variety of applications. However, RNNs can be difficult and slow to train.

Researchers are working on a number of ways to address the challenges of RNNs. One promising approach is to use gated recurrent units (GRUs) and long short-term memory (LSTM) units. These units are designed to address the vanishing gradient problem and make RNNs easier to train.

Another promising approach is to use attention mechanisms. Attention mechanisms allow RNNs to focus on the most important parts of the sequence of data. This can make RNNs faster and more efficient.

RNNs are a rapidly evolving field of research. As new techniques are developed, RNNs are likely to become even more powerful and versatile tools for processing sequential data.

The Essence of Sequential Data

Sequential data is a common form of data in which each data point is not independent but influenced by the previous ones. Examples of sequential data include time series data, where each data point depends on the previous one, and natural language, where the meaning of a word or phrase is heavily influenced by the words that precede it.

In essence, RNNs are designed to capture and leverage these dependencies. They are equipped with hidden states that allow them to maintain memory of the past, making them suitable for tasks that require understanding and prediction of sequences.

The Architecture of RNNs

The fundamental building block of an RNN is the recurrent neuron. This neuron maintains a hidden state, which serves as its memory. At each time step, the neuron takes an input, combines it with its hidden state, and produces an output and an updated hidden state. This process is recurrent, as the hidden state at the current time step depends on the hidden state at the previous time step.

This recurrent structure allows RNNs to model sequences of variable length. However, it also poses challenges, such as vanishing gradients, which can hinder their ability to capture long range dependencies effectively.

Types of RNNs

Several variations of RNNs have been developed to address the challenges posed by the simple RNN architecture. Notable types of RNNs include:

Long Short Term Memory (LSTM): LSTMs are designed to alleviate the vanishing gradient problem by introducing specialized memory cells. These cells can learn when to remember and when to forget information, making LSTMs highly effective in capturing long range dependencies.

Gated Recurrent Unit (GRU): GRUs are similar to LSTMs but have a simplified structure with two gates an update gate and a reset gate. They offer a balance between performance and computational efficiency.

1.3.4 Transformers Models

Transformers represent a groundbreaking advancement in the field of natural language processing and beyond. These architectures have revolutionized the way we process sequential data, with applications ranging from machine translation to text summarization. In this section, we explore the core concepts of Transformers and delve into two pioneering models, BERT and GPT.

Transformer models were first introduced in the paper "Attention is All You Need" by Vaswani et al. in 2017, and they have since become the state-of-the-art for many NLP tasks, including machine translation, text summarization, and question answering.

Transformer models are based on a self-attention mechanism, which allows them to learn long-range dependencies in sequential data. This makes transformer models well-suited for NLP tasks, which often require the model to understand the relationships between words that are far apart in the sequence.

Transformer models are typically made up of two main components: an encoder and a decoder. The encoder takes the input sequence and produces a hidden representation of the sequence. The decoder then takes the hidden representation of the sequence and produces the output sequence.

The self-attention mechanism is used in both the encoder and decoder. In the encoder, the self-attention mechanism allows the model to learn the relationships between different parts of the input sequence. In the decoder, the self-attention mechanism allows the model to learn the relationships between different parts of the output sequence and the hidden representation of the input sequence.

Transformer models have been shown to achieve state-of-the-art results on many NLP tasks, including:

- Machine translation: Transformer models have outperformed previous state-of-the-art methods on many machine translation benchmarks.

- Text summarization: Transformer models have also outperformed previous state-of-the-art methods on many text summarization benchmarks.

- Question answering: Transformer models have been shown to be effective for question answering tasks, such as the SQuAD benchmark.

In addition to these tasks, transformer models have also been used for other NLP tasks, such as natural language inference, sentiment analysis, and text generation.

Transformer models have had a major impact on the field of NLP. They have allowed researchers to achieve state-of-the-art results on many challenging NLP tasks. Transformer models are now used in a wide variety of commercial and open-source applications.

Advantages of transformer models

Transformer models have a number of advantages over previous NLP models, including:

- Ability to learn long-range dependencies: Transformer models are able to learn long-range dependencies in sequential data, which makes them well-suited for NLP tasks.

- Parallelism: Transformer models can be parallelized, which makes them faster to train and deploy.

- Generality: Transformer models can be used for a wide variety of NLP tasks, such as machine translation, text summarization, and question answering.

Disadvantages of transformer models

Transformer models also have some disadvantages, including:

- Complexity: Transformer models can be complex to train and deploy.

- Resource requirements: Transformer models require a lot of computational resources to train and deploy.

Applications of transformer models

Transformer models are used in a wide variety of commercial and open-source applications, including:

- Machine translation: Transformer models are used in machine translation services such as Google Translate and Microsoft Translator.

- Text summarization: Transformer models are used in text summarization tools such as Google Bard and Microsoft Bing Summarization.

- Question answering: Transformer models are used in question answering systems such as Google Search and Amazon Alexa.

- Natural language inference: Transformer models are used in natural language inference systems such as the Stanford NLI Corpus.

- Sentiment analysis: Transformer models are used in sentiment analysis systems such as Google Cloud Natural Language and Amazon Rekognition.

- Text generation: Transformer models are used in text generation systems such as Google Bard and GPT-3.

Conclusion

Transformer models are a powerful new type of neural network architecture that has revolutionized the field of NLP. Transformer models have been shown to achieve state-of-the-art results on many challenging NLP tasks, and they are now used in a wide variety of commercial and open-source applications.

The Transformer Architecture

The Transformer architecture, introduced by Vaswani et al. in their 2017 paper "Attention is All You Need," marked a shift away from recurrent and convolutional neural networks for sequence to sequence tasks. At its core, the Transformer architecture relies on self attention mechanisms that enable it to weigh the significance of different parts of the input sequence. This innovation allowed Transformers to process sequences in parallel rather than sequentially.

Key components of the Transformer architecture include:

Multi Head Self Attention Mechanism: This mechanism enables the model to focus on different parts of the input sequence simultaneously. It computes weighted sums of input sequence elements to generate context aware representations.

Positional Encoding: Transformers lack an inherent sense of position in sequences, so positional encodings are added to the input embeddings to provide information about the order of words in the sequence.

FeedForward Networks: After attention mechanisms, the model employs feedforward networks to further process the information.

Layer Normalization: This technique helps stabilize training by normalizing activations.

Stacked Layers: Transformers consist of multiple layers stacked on top of each other, enabling the model to learn hierarchical representations.

Variants of Transformer Models

Transformer models are a type of neural network architecture that has revolutionized the field of natural language processing (NLP). Transformer models were first introduced in the paper "Attention is All You Need" by Vaswani et al. in 2017, and they have since become the state-of-the-art for many NLP tasks, including machine translation, text summarization, and question answering.

Over the past few years, a number of variants of transformer models have been developed. Some of the most popular variants of transformer models include:

- BERT (Bidirectional Encoder Representations from Transformers): BERT is a pre-trained transformer model that was introduced by Google AI in 2018. BERT is typically used for tasks such as question answering, text classification, and natural language inference.

- BART (Bidirectional and Autoregressive Transformers): BART is a pre-trained transformer model that was introduced by Facebook AI in 2020. BART is typically used for tasks such as machine translation, text summarization, and question answering.

Here is a table that summarizes the key differences between BERT and BART:

Feature	BERT	BART
Model type	Bidirectional encoder	Bidirectional encoder-decoder
Pre-training task	Masked language modeling	Sequence-to-sequence de-noising
Typical downstream tasks	Question answering, text classification, natural language inference	Machine translation, text summarization, question answering

- GPT-3 (Generative Pre-trained Transformer 3):

GPT-3 is a pre-trained transformer model that was introduced by OpenAI in 2020. GPT-3 is typically used for tasks such as text generation, translation, and summarization. GPT, introduced by Radford et al. in "Improving Language Understanding by Generative Pre-training," is another influential pre-trained Transformer model. Unlike BERT, GPT is "unidirectional" and focuses on autoregressive language modeling, predicting the next word in a sequence based on the preceding words.

GPT's generative capabilities have been leveraged for text generation tasks, including story writing, poetry, and code generation. GPT models have the ability to produce coherent and contextually relevant text, making them a valuable tool in creative content generation.

- RoBERTa (A Robustly Optimized BERT Pre-training Approach): RoBERTa is a pre-trained transformer model that was introduced by Facebook AI in 2020. RoBERTa is a more robust version of BERT, and it has been shown to achieve state-of-the-art results on many NLP tasks.

- DistilBERT: DistilBERT is a smaller and faster version of BERT. DistilBERT is typically used for tasks where performance is more important than speed, such as mobile applications.

These are just a few of the many variants of transformer models that have been developed. Researchers are constantly developing new variants of transformer models, and it is likely that new variants will continue to be developed in the future.

Transformer models have a number of advantages over previous NLP models, including:

- Ability to learn long-range dependencies: Transformer models are able to learn long-range dependencies in sequential data, which makes them well-suited for NLP tasks.

- Parallelism: Transformer models can be parallelized, which makes them faster to train and deploy.

- Generality: Transformer models can be used for a wide variety of NLP tasks, such as machine translation, text summarization, and question answering.

Transformer models have had a major impact on the field of NLP. They have allowed researchers to achieve state-of-the-art results on many challenging NLP tasks. Transformer models are now used in a wide variety of commercial and open-source applications.

Conclusion

Transformer models and their variants are powerful tools for natural language processing. They have revolutionized the field and are now used in a wide variety of applications. As research in this area

Chapter 2 A Deeper Dive into Deep Learning Models

2.1 Introduction:

In this section, we will explore a simplified deep learning model with various layers, providing mathematical equations and calculations for each layer. Furthermore, we will apply this model to a sample dataset and calculate the model's output.

A simplified deep learning model with various layers might look like this:

Input layer -> Hidden layer 1 -> Hidden layer 2 -> Output layer

The input layer takes the input data and passes it on to the hidden layers. The hidden layers process the data and learn to extract features from the data. The output layer takes the output of the hidden layers and produces the final prediction.

2.1.1 Technical Ground of Deep Learning

Deep learning is a type of machine learning that uses artificial neural networks to learn from data. Neural networks are inspired by the structure and function of the human brain, and they are made up of interconnected nodes, called neurons, which process information and pass it on to other neurons. Neural networks can be trained to perform a wide variety of tasks, including image recognition, natural language processing, and machine translation.

One of the key advantages of deep learning is its ability to learn from data. Deep learning models do not need to be explicitly programmed to perform a task. Instead, they can be trained on a dataset of examples, and they will learn to perform the task by identifying patterns in the data.

Another advantage of deep learning is its ability to generalize to new data. Deep learning models do not overfit the training data, meaning that they can generalize to new data that they have never seen before. This makes deep learning models well-suited for real-world applications, where the data is often noisy and variable.

Simplified Deep Learning Model

A simplified deep learning model with various layers might look like this:

Input layer -> Hidden layer 1 -> Hidden layer 2 -> Output layer

Mathematical Equations

The following mathematical equations describe the forward pass through a simplified deep learning model with two hidden layers:

Output of the first hidden layer:

$h1 = f(W1 * x + b1)$

Output of the second hidden layer:

$h2 = f(W2 * h1 + b2)$

Output of the output layer:

$o = f(W3 * h2 + b3)$

where:

- x is the input data

- W1, W2, and W3 are the weights of the first, second, and third layers, respectively

- b1, b2, and b3 are the biases of the first, second, and third layers, respectively

- f is the activation function

The activation function is a non-linear function that is used to add non-linearity to the model. This allows the model to learn more complex patterns in the data.

1. Input Layer

The input layer takes the raw data and feeds it into the neural network. Suppose we have a dataset with one input feature (e.g., a numerical value), and we have one data point to process. The input data can be represented as follows:

Input Data (X): 5.0

2. Fully Connected (Dense) Layer

The input layer takes the input data and passes it on to the hidden layers. The hidden layers process the data and learn to extract features from the data. The output layer takes the output of the hidden layers and produces the final prediction.

The fully connected layer, often referred to as the dense layer, performs a linear transformation of the input data using weights and biases. The output can be calculated as follows:

Input Data (X): 5.0

Weights (W1): 2.0

Bias (b1): 1.0

Output from the dense layer:

Output (O1) = (X W1) + b1

Output (O1) = (5.0 2.0) + 1.0 = 11.0

3. Activation Function (ReLU) Layer

After the dense layer, an activation function, in this case, the Rectified Linear Unit (ReLU) function, is applied elementwise to introduce nonlinearity into the model:

Output from Dense Layer (O1): 11.0

Output after applying ReLU activation function:

Output (O2) = max(0, O1) = max(0, 11.0) = 11.0

4. Fully Connected (Dense) Layer

Let's add another fully connected layer with new weights and biases:

Weights (W2): 3.0

Bias (b2): 2.0

Output from the previous layer (ReLU output):

Output from ReLU Layer (O2): 11.0

Output from the dense layer:

Output (O3) = (O2 W2) + b2

Output (O3) = (11.0 3.0) + 2.0 = 35.0

5. Output Layer

The final layer produces the model's output, which may depend on the specific task (e.g., regression or classification). In this example, we'll consider a regression task. The output can be calculated as follows:

Output from Dense Layer (O3): 35.0

Final output from the model:

Output (Final) = O3 = 35.0

Example: Application to a Sample Dataset

Now, let's apply this simplified deep learning model to a sample dataset. Consider the following dataset:

Input(X)	Output (Y)
1.0	5.0
2.0	8.0
3.0	11.0
4.0	14.0

We'll use the model described above to make predictions for this dataset:

1. For `Input (X) = 1.0`, the model predicts `Output (Y) = 35.0`.

2. For `Input (X) = 2.0`, the model predicts `Output (Y) = 35.0`.

3. For `Input (X) = 3.0`, the model predicts `Output (Y) = 35.0`.

4. For `Input (X) = 4.0`, the model predicts `Output (Y) = 35.0`.

In this simplified example, the model's predictions are constant and do not capture the true relationship in the data. However, in practice, deep learning models with more complex architectures and larger datasets are capable of learning meaningful patterns and making accurate predictions.

2.1.2 Feature Generation Layer by Layer:

In the simplified deep learning model described in Section 5, feature vectors are generated as the output of the various layers in the model. Each layer in the neural network transforms the input data into a new representation, which can be thought of as a feature vector. Let's break down how feature vectors are generated in this model:

1. Input Layer: The initial input data (X) serves as the first feature vector. In the example, this is simply the input value (e.g., X = 5.0).

2. Fully Connected (Dense) Layer 1: The first dense layer takes the input feature vector and applies a linear transformation using weights (W1) and a bias (b1). The output (O1) from this layer is a new feature vector generated by combining and transforming the input. In the example, O1 is the first feature vector produced (e.g., O1 = 11.0).

3. Activation Function (ReLU) Layer: The ReLU activation function is applied to the output of the previous layer (O1). This introduces nonlinearity into the model, and the output (O2) of this layer is another feature vector. In this case, O2 is simply the ReLU applied to O1 (e.g., O2 = max(0, O1) = 11.0).

4. Fully Connected (Dense) Layer 2: The second dense layer further transforms the feature vector produced by the ReLU layer (O2) using a different set of weights (W2) and a bias (b2). The output (O3) of this layer is yet another feature vector generated by this transformation (e.g., O3 = 35.0).

5. Output Layer: The final layer in the model, in this case, the output layer, produces the model's final feature vector or output. The output of the previous layer (O3) is used as the feature vector for this layer (e.g., O3 = 35.0).

In this simplified example, the feature vectors evolve as the input data goes through each layer of the model. The final feature vector (O3) produced by the output layer represents the model's prediction or output for the given input.

In practical deep learning models, these feature vectors often contain higher dimensional representations and capture more complex patterns in the data. These representations are learned during the training process, enabling the model to make accurate predictions or perform various tasks based on the input data.

Example o Real World Application:

let's apply the simplified deep learning model to a real world example dataset. In this case, we'll work with a regression task where the goal is to predict house prices based on a single input feature (e.g., the number of bedrooms). We will use the model's architecture described in Section 5. I'll use some arbitrary values for the model's weights and biases to demonstrate the step-by-step process.

Dataset:

Number of Bedrooms (X)	House Price (Y)
2	200000
3	250000
4	300000
5	350000

Model Architecture:

1. Input Layer: Passes the number of bedrooms (X) directly to the first dense layer.

2. Fully Connected (Dense) Layer 1: Applies a linear transformation:

Weight (W1) = 10,000

Bias (b1) = 50,000

Output (O1) = (X W1) + b1

3. Activation Function (ReLU) Layer: Applies ReLU activation.

Output (O2) = max(0, O1)

4. Fully Connected (Dense) Layer 2: Applies a linear transformation:

Weight (W2) = 5,000

Bias (b2) = 100,000

Output (O3) = (O2 W2) + b2

5. Output Layer: The output from the second dense layer (O3) is the model's prediction for the house price.

Step by Step Calculation for a Single Data Point:

Let's calculate the predicted house price for a house with 3 bedrooms (X = 3).

1. Input Layer:

X = 3

2. Fully Connected (Dense) Layer 1:

W1 = 10,000

b1 = 50,000

O1 = (3 10,000) + 50,000 = 80,000

3. Activation Function (ReLU) Layer:

O2 = max(0, 80,000) = 80,000

4. Fully Connected (Dense) Layer 2:

W2 = 5,000

b2 = 100,000

O3 = (80,000 5,000) + 100,000 = 500,000 + 100,000 = 600,000

5. Output Layer:

The final prediction for the house price (Y) is O3 = 600,000

So, for a house with 3 bedrooms, the model predicts a house price of $600,000.

You can follow the same steps for other data points in the dataset to calculate the model's predictions for each of them. This demonstrates how the model's architecture processes the input feature to make predictions based on the weights and biases of the various layers.

2.1.3 Deep Learning Training Process

Deep learning training is the process of teaching a deep learning model to perform a task by feeding it data and allowing it to learn from the data. The training process is iterative, meaning that the model is repeatedly presented with the data and its predictions are adjusted until the model is able to perform the task accurately.

Technical Formulation

The deep learning training process can be formulated as an optimization problem. The goal of the training process is to minimize the loss function, which is a measure of how far the model's predictions are from the ground truth labels. The loss function is typically minimized using a gradient descent algorithm, which iteratively updates the model's parameters in the direction of decreasing loss.

The following mathematical equation describes the update rule for the gradient descent algorithm:

$$\theta \leftarrow \theta - \alpha * \nabla L(\theta)$$

where:

- θ is the model's parameters

- α is the learning rate

- $\nabla L(\theta)$ is the gradient of the loss function with respect to the model's parameters

The learning rate is a hyper parameter that controls how quickly the model learns. A higher learning rate will cause the model to learn more quickly, but it may also cause the model to become unstable. A lower learning rate will cause the model to learn more slowly, but it will also make the model more stable.

Examination of the Deep Learning Training Process

There are a number of factors that can affect the success of the deep learning training process, including:

- The quality and quantity of the training data: The training data should be representative of the data that the model will be used on in production. Additionally, the more training data that is available, the better the model will be able to learn.

- The architecture of the neural network: The architecture of the neural network will determine the model's ability to learn complex patterns in the data. A more complex architecture will allow the model to learn more complex patterns, but it will also make the model more difficult to train.

- The hyper parameters of the training process: The hyper parameters of the training process, such as the learning rate and the number of training epochs, can also affect the success of the training process. It is important to experiment with different hyper parameters to find the values that work best for the specific problem that is being solved.

The deep learning training process is a complex process that can be affected by a number of factors. However, by understanding the basic principles of deep learning training and by carefully considering the factors that can affect the training process, it is possible to train deep learning models that can achieve state-of-the-art results on a wide variety of problems.

In addition to the factors mentioned above, there are a number of other things that can be done to improve the success of the deep learning training process, such as:

- Using regularization techniques: Regularization techniques can help to prevent the model from over-fitting the training data.

- Using data augmentation: Data augmentation techniques can be used to increase the size and diversity of the training data.

- Using transfer learning: Transfer learning techniques can be used to initialize the model's parameters with values that have already been learned on a related task.

By following these best practices, it is possible to train deep learning models that are more accurate, more efficient, and more robust.

Explanation of Mathematical Model:

The mathematical formula for training a deep learning model typically involves the following key components:

1. Loss Function (L): This function quantifies the error or discrepancy between the model's predictions and the actual target values. The choice of the loss function depends on the specific task (e.g., mean squared error for regression, cross entropy for classification).

2. Model Parameters (θ): These are the weights and biases of the neural network that need to be learned during training.

3. Training Data (X): This is the input data, and for supervised learning, it's typically a matrix with one row per example and one column per feature.

4. Learning Rate (α): This is a hyper parameter that determines the step size for updating the model parameters during training.

The training process can be mathematically described using gradient descent, a common optimization algorithm for deep learning. Here's the basic formula for one iteration(one training step) of gradient descent:

1. Forward Pass (Prediction):

Calculate the model's prediction ($\hat{y}$) for the given input (X) using the current model parameters (θ).

$\hat{y} = \text{Model}(X, \theta)$

2. Loss Calculation:

Calculate the loss (L) by comparing the model's prediction (ŷ) to the actual target values (Y) using the chosen loss function (L).

$$L = Loss(ŷ, Y)$$

3. Back propagation (Gradient Calculation):

Compute the gradient of the loss with respect to the model parameters. This is done by taking the partial derivative of the loss with respect to each model parameter.

$$\nabla L/\nabla \theta = \partial L/\partial \theta$$

4. Parameter Update:

Update the model parameters (θ) using the gradient information and the learning rate (α). The specific update rule depends on the optimization algorithm (e.g., gradient descent, Adam, RMSprop).

$$\theta = \theta\ \alpha\ \nabla L/\nabla \theta$$

5. Repeat:

Repeat steps 1 to 4 for a specified number of training iterations (epochs) or until a convergence criterion is met.

The goal of training is to minimize the loss function by iteratively updating the model parameters. This process is called gradient descent, and it helps the model learn to make better predictions. Training continues until the loss converges to a minimum value, indicating that the model has learned the underlying patterns in the data.

In practice, deep learning frameworks, such as TensorFlow and PyTorch, handle the mathematical details of these calculations, so you don't need to implement them from scratch. However, understanding the fundamental equations is essential for effectively tuning and troubleshooting deep learning models.

2.1.4 Maintenance of Training Set

In deep learning, the data of the training set is maintained and used by the model during the training process to learn patterns, adjust model parameters (weights and biases), and make predictions. The data is typically organized and processed in mini batches. Here's how the model maintains and utilizes the training data:

1. Data Loading:

The training data is initially loaded into memory or accessed from storage. This data consists of pairs of input features (X) and corresponding target values or labels (Y).

2. Data Splitting:

The training dataset is often divided into smaller subsets called mini batches. The mini batches are randomly sampled from the training data, ensuring that each example is included in one or more mini batches. This randomization helps prevent the model from learning the order of the data.

3. Mini Batch Processing:

During training, the model processes one mini batch at a time. Each mini batch contains a set of input features (X) and their corresponding target values (Y).

The model uses the input features (X) to make predictions ($\hat{y}$) for that mini batch.

4. Loss Calculation:

After making predictions, the model calculates the loss (L) by comparing its predictions ($\hat{y}$) to the true target values (Y). The loss function quantifies the error for that mini batch.

5. Back Propagation and Parameter Updates:

The gradients of the loss with respect to the model parameters (weights and biases) are computed using the mini batch. This involves taking the partial derivatives of the loss with respect to each parameter.

The model parameters are updated using the gradients and an optimization algorithm (e.g., stochastic gradient descent). This step is critical for the model to learn from the data.

6. Iterative Process:

The model repeats the process of processing mini batches, calculating loss, and updating parameters for a specified number of training iterations (epochs) or until a convergence criterion is met.

Each iteration involves a different mini batch from the training data.

7. Shuffling and Repeat:

After each complete pass through the training data (one epoch), the order of the mini batches is often shuffled to introduce randomness and prevent over fitting.

The process of iterating through the training data is repeated until the model converges or a predefined stopping criterion is met.

8. Model Learning:

As the model processes different mini batches, it learns to make better predictions and adjust its parameters. Over time, it captures patterns and relationships in the data.

By maintaining and processing data in mini batches, the model efficiently learns from large datasets, benefits from parallelization (which speeds up training on modern hardware), and can generalize to unseen data. This iterative process of mini batch training continues until the model reaches a satisfactory level of performance.

Data Representation

Data representation in the context of training deep learning models is a critical aspect of how the model interprets and processes the input data. Deep learning models often work with numerical representations of data, and these representations can take various forms, including vectors, matrices, and tensors. Here's an explanation of these different data representations:

1. Vector Representation:

A vector is a one dimensional array of numerical values. In the context of deep learning, it is often used to represent individual data points or features.

For example, in a simple text classification task, a document can be represented as a vector where each element of the vector corresponds to the frequency of a specific word in the document. This results in a high dimensional feature vector.

2. Matrix Representation:

A matrix is a two dimensional grid of numerical values. In deep learning, matrices are commonly used to represent datasets where each row corresponds to a data point, and each column corresponds to a feature or attribute.

In image processing, for instance, an image can be represented as a matrix where each element represents the pixel intensity.

3. Tensor Representation:

A tensor is a multidimensional array. In deep learning, tensors are used to represent more complex data structures, such as multichannel images, time series data, or sequences of data.

For example, a color image can be represented as a three dimensional tensor, with dimensions representing height, width, and color channels (e.g., red, green, blue).

4. Sequence Representation:

In natural language processing and sequential data tasks, sequences of data are commonly represented as lists or arrays of vectors. Each element in the sequence corresponds to a data point at a specific time step.

5. Sparse Representation:

Some data is inherently sparse, meaning that most of the elements are zero. For example, in text data, a document term matrix can be highly sparse because most words do not appear in a given document. Sparse representations are often used to save memory and improve efficiency.

6. Embedding Representation:

Embeddings are low dimensional vector representations of objects or entities. In natural language processing, word embeddings (e.g., Word2Vec, GloVe) are widely used to represent words as continuous valued vectors in a lower dimensional space.

Data representation is a fundamental aspect of deep learning, and choosing the right representation depends on the nature of the data and the specific task. Deep learning frameworks and libraries, such as TensorFlow and PyTorch, provide tools and functions for efficiently working with these different data representations, making it easier to build and train deep learning models on diverse types of data.

Simplified Example of Data Representation:

1. Vector Representation:
 Example: Word Frequency Vector

Consider a document containing the words "cat," "dog," "house," and "tree."

A vector representation for this document might be `[3, 2, 1, 0]`, where each element represents the frequency of a specific word in the document. In this case, "cat" appears 3 times, "dog" appears 2 times, "house" appears 1 time, and "tree" does not appear.

2. Matrix Representation:
Example: Image Pixel Matrix

An RGB image can be represented as a matrix where each element contains the intensity values for the red, green, and blue color channels at a specific pixel location. For instance, a 32x32pixel color image can be represented as a 32x32x3 matrix, with each element containing the color intensity values.

3. Tensor Representation:
 Example: Video Frames

A video can be represented as a four dimensional tensor with dimensions for frame number, height, width, and color channels. For a color video with a resolution of 720p (1280x720 pixels), each frame is represented as a 1280x720x3 tensor.

4. Sequence Representation:
 Example: Time Series Data

Financial time series data, such as stock prices over time, can be represented as a sequence of vectors. Each vector contains data for a specific time step, and the entire time series is a list of such vectors.

5. Sparse Representation:
Example: Document Term Matrix

In natural language processing, a document term matrix represents a collection of documents and the frequency of words within them. Most entries in this matrix are zero, as most words do not appear in most documents. It is typically a sparse matrix.

6. Embedding Representation:
Example: Word Embeddings

Word embeddings represent words as dense vectors in a continuous valued space. For example, "king" and "queen" may be represented as vectors with specific numerical values, capturing semantic relationships between words.

These data representations are used in various deep learning tasks, including natural language processing, computer vision, time series analysis, and more. Choosing the appropriate representation depends on the nature of the data and the specific requirements of the deep learning task.

Example: Let train the model by 20 pictures of cats. How the model will be trained and how many vectors will be created? How many values will be stored in each vector?

Ans: When training a deep learning model to classify images of cats, the process typically involves the following steps, assuming you have a dataset of 20 images of cats:

1. Data Preparation: The 20 cat images are collected, and each image is resized to a consistent size (e.g., 224x224 pixels) to ensure uniformity.

The images are often converted to numerical representations. This is commonly done using RGB pixel values for color images. Each image is represented as a three dimensional matrix (tensor), with dimensions for width, height, and color channels (usually red, green, and blue).

2. Feature Extraction: Feature extraction may be performed to capture relevant information from the images. For example, you could use pre-trained convolutional neural networks (CNNs) to extract features from the images. These features can be considered as numerical vectors representing the images.

3. Vector Representation: Each image's feature representation results in a vector. This vector typically contains a large number of values. For instance, if you use a pre-trained CNN model like VGG16 or ResNet, the feature vector might have thousands of values per image.

4. Training Data: These feature vectors, one for each image, constitute the training data for your model. You now have 20 feature vectors, one for each cat image.

5. Labeling: You also need to label your training data. For each image, you need to specify whether it's a cat (label 1) or not a cat (label 0). This labeling allows your model to learn to distinguish between cat images and noncat images.

6. Model Architecture: Define the architecture of your deep learning model, which could be a neural network designed for image classification.

7. Training: Train your model using the labeled feature vectors as input. The model will learn to recognize patterns in the vectors that are associated with cat images.

8. Evaluation: After training, you can evaluate your model's performance on new, unseen images to assess its accuracy in classifying cat images.

The number of values stored in each feature vector depends on the complexity of the feature extraction method used. A typical pre-trained deep neural network might result in feature vectors with thousands of values per image. These vectors capture high level features and representations of the images, such as edges, textures, and more.

It's worth noting that when you have a small dataset like 20 images, the model may not perform as well as it could with a larger dataset. Deep learning models often require a large amount of data to generalize effectively. Techniques like data augmentation, transfer learning, and regularization can be employed to improve performance with limited data.

2.1.5 Implementation in Python:

There's a simple example of a deep learning model implemented in Python using the popular deep learning library, TensorFlow. This example demonstrates a basic feed forward neural network for binary classification. Make sure you have TensorFlow installed (you can install it via `pip install tensorflow`).

```
import tensorflow as tf
import numpy as np
# Generate some random training data (20 data points)
np.random.seed(0)
X = np.random.rand(20, 2)
Y = (X[:, 0] + X[:, 1] > 1).astype(int)  # Binary classification task
# Define the model
model = tf.keras.Sequential([
    tf.keras.layers.Dense(10, activation='relu', input_shape=(2,)),
    tf.keras.layers.Dense(1, activation='sigmoid')
])
# Compile the model
model.compile(optimizer='adam',
        loss='binary_crossentropy',
        metrics=['accuracy'])
# Train the model
model.fit(X, Y, epochs=100)
# Evaluate the model
loss, accuracy = model.evaluate(X, Y)
print(f'Loss: {loss}, Accuracy: {accuracy}')
# Make predictions
predictions = model.predict(X)
print("Predictions:")
print(predictions)
```

In this code:

1. We generate some random training data `X` (features) and `Y` (binary labels) for a binary classification task.

2. We define a simple feed forward neural network model using TensorFlow's `tf.keras.Sequential` API. It has an input layer with 2 units (for the 2 features), a hidden layer with 10 units and ReLU activation, and an output layer with 1 unit and a sigmoid activation function for binary classification.

3. We compile the model, specifying the optimizer (Adam), loss function (binary cross entropy), and evaluation metric (accuracy).

4. We train the model on the training data for 100 epochs.

5. We evaluate the model on the same training data to check its performance.

30

6. We make predictions using the trained model.

This code is a basic example to get you started with deep learning using TensorFlow. For more complex tasks and real world datasets, you would typically need a larger, more complex model and potentially additional techniques like data preprocessing, data augmentation, and model tuning.

Example: How to deploy a trained Model.?

Ans: Deploying a trained deep learning model involves making your model available for use in a production environment, such as a web application or a server. The specific steps to deploy a model can vary depending on the framework and tools you are using. Here is a general guideline for deploying a trained model:

1. Export or Save the Model:

Save the trained model and its associated weights and architecture to a file. Most deep learning frameworks allow you to save models in formats such as TensorFlow's Saved Model format, PyTorch's .pt files, or ONNX format. This allows you to load the model for deployment.

2. Choose a Deployment Environment:

Decide where you want to deploy the model. Common deployment environments include cloud services (e.g., AWS, Azure, Google Cloud), on premises servers, or edge devices (e.g., mobile devices or IoT devices).

3. Set Up the Deployment Environment:

Depending on your chosen environment, set up the necessary infrastructure and resources. This may include configuring a server, setting up virtual machines, or deploying to a cloud service.

4. Model Inference Code:

Write or adapt code to perform model inference in your deployment environment. This code should load the saved model, preprocess input data, make predictions, and post process the results if necessary.

5. API or Application Integration:

Integrate the model inference code into your application or service. This may involve creating APIs or web services to expose the model's predictions, or embedding the model within an application.

6. Scaling and Performance Optimization:

Ensure that your deployment can handle the expected load. You may need to scale the deployment infrastructure to meet the performance requirements. Techniques like load balancing and caching can be useful.

7. Security:

Implement security measures to protect your deployed model from potential threats. This includes access control, input validation, and potentially using encryption for data transfer.

8. Monitoring and Logging:

Set up monitoring and logging to track the performance and health of your deployed model. This helps you identify issues and improve the model over time.

9. Testing and Quality Assurance:

Before going live, thoroughly test the deployed model. Test it with a variety of inputs and edge cases to ensure it performs as expected.

10. Versioning:

Implement versioning for your models so that you can manage and switch between different model versions easily.

11. Documentation:

Document the usage of the deployed model, including input and output formats, API endpoints, and any relevant instructions.

12. Deployment and Maintenance:

Deploy the model to your chosen environment and continuously monitor its performance. Be prepared to update the model as needed based on new data or changes in the application's requirements.

13. Scalability and Load Testing:

Continuously assess the scalability and performance of your deployed model. You may need to optimize or scale your deployment as usage grows.

The deployment process can be complex, and the specifics can vary based on the technology stack, domain, and deployment environment. Be sure to follow best practices and consider issues like security, scalability, and performance to ensure your deployed model operates reliably and efficiently in a production setting.

Using Deep Learning Model for Image Classification

Using deep learning models for image classification is a common and powerful application of deep learning. Here's a step by step guide on how to do it:

1. Data Preparation:

Gather a dataset of labeled images. Ensure that the dataset is well organized, with images grouped into different classes or categories.

Split the dataset into training, validation, and test sets. Typically, you'll use a larger portion of the data for training and smaller portions for validation and testing.

2. Data Preprocessing:

Resize the images to a consistent size (e.g., 224x224 pixels) to ensure uniform input size for the model.

Normalize the pixel values to a common scale (e.g., [0, 1] or [1, 1]).

Augment the data if needed. Data augmentation techniques include random rotations, flips, and translations, which increase the diversity of the training data.

3. Model Selection:

Choose a deep learning model architecture suitable for image classification. Common choices include Convolutional Neural Networks (CNNs) like VGG, ResNet, Inception, and custom architectures.

You can use pre-trained models as a starting point for transfer learning. Pre-trained models trained on large image datasets like ImageNet can provide a good foundation.

4. Model Building:

Build the selected model using a deep learning framework (e.g., TensorFlow, PyTorch). Customize the model architecture as needed.

If using transfer learning, remove the top classification layers and add new layers specific to your task.

5. Model Compilation:

Compile the model by specifying the optimizer, loss function, and evaluation metrics. For image classification, a common choice is the categorical cross entropy loss function.

6. Model Training:

Train the model on the training dataset. The model learns to recognize patterns and features in the images by adjusting its parameters (weights and biases).

Monitor the model's performance on the validation set to detect over-fitting- and fine-tune hyper parameters.

7. Model Evaluation:

Evaluate the trained model on the test dataset to assess its performance. Metrics such as accuracy, precision, recall, and F1 score can be used to measure classification performance.

8. Inference:

Once the model is trained and evaluated, you can use it for making predictions on new, unseen images.

Preprocess input images as you did during training, and pass them through the model for inference.

9. Deployment:

Deploy the trained model in a production environment, such as a web service or mobile application, as explained in the previous answer.

10. Monitoring and Maintenance:

Continuously monitor the model's performance and retrain it with new data if necessary.

Periodically update the model to improve its performance or adapt to changing requirements.

This general process outlines the steps for using a deep learning model for image classification. The choice of the specific model architecture, data preprocessing, and hyper parameters will depend on the nature of your image classification task. Additionally, fine-tuning and experimentation may be required to achieve the best results.

Python code for Image Classification Using Deep Learning Model:
Creating a deep learning model for image classification is a detailed process, and the code can be quite extensive. However, I'll provide a simple example of building a Convolutional Neural Network (CNN) for image classification using TensorFlow and Keras. This example assumes you have a dataset of images prepared and organized for classification. You'll need to adapt the code to your specific dataset and requirements.

Please make sure you have TensorFlow and any required libraries installed. You can install TensorFlow via `pip install tensorflow`.

```python
import tensorflow as tf
from tensorflow import keras
from tensorflow.keras import layers
# Define the CNN model
model = keras.Sequential([
    layers.Conv2D(32, (3, 3), activation='relu', input_shape=(224, 224, 3)),
    layers.MaxPooling2D((2, 2)),
    layers.Conv2D(64, (3, 3), activation='relu'),
    layers.MaxPooling2D((2, 2)),
    layers.Conv2D(64, (3, 3), activation='relu'),
    layers.Flatten(),
```

```
    layers.Dense(64, activation='relu'),
    layers.Dense(10, activation='softmax')  # Adjust the number of classes as needed
])

# Compile the model
model.compile(optimizer='adam',
         loss='sparse_categorical_crossentropy',
         metrics=['accuracy'])

# Load and preprocess your dataset
# For demonstration purposes, let's assume you have X_train and y_train

# Train the model
model.fit(X_train, y_train, epochs=10)  # Adjust the number of epochs as needed

# Evaluate the model on a validation set
# For demonstration purposes, let's assume you have X_val and y_val
val_loss, val_accuracy = model.evaluate(X_val, y_val)
print(f'Validation loss: {val_loss}, Validation accuracy: {val_accuracy}')

# Make predictions on new data
# For demonstration purposes, let's assume you have X_test
predictions = model.predict(X_test)
```

In This Code

We define a simple CNN model using the Keras Sequential API. This model consists of convolutional layers, max pooling layers, and fully connected layers.

- The `model.compile` step specifies the optimizer, loss function, and evaluation metric.
- You would need to load and preprocess your image dataset. The input shape `(224, 224, 3)` assumes RGB color images with a size of 224x224 pixels.
- We train the model using your training data (`X_train` and `y_train`) for a specified number of epochs.
- We evaluate the model's performance on a validation set (`X_val` and `y_val`) to check its accuracy.
- Finally, we make predictions on new data using the `model.predict` function.

Please note that this is a basic example, and for real world tasks, you may need to handle data augmentation, perform more extensive data preprocessing, fine tune hyper parameters, and potentially use transfer learning with pre-trained models. The specific details and adjustments will depend on your dataset and task.

Sentiment Analysis Using RNN

Sentiment analysis is a common natural language processing (NLP) task, and deep learning models like recurrent neural networks (RNNs) or transformers can be used for this purpose. Here's a Python code example for applying a deep learning model for sentiment analysis using TensorFlow and Keras. This code assumes you have a labeled dataset of product reviews where each review is labeled as positive or negative.

Please make sure you have TensorFlow installed (`pip install tensorflow`) and, if necessary, a preprocessed dataset in a suitable format for training and evaluation.

```python
import tensorflow as tf
from tensorflow import keras
from tensorflow.keras.preprocessing.text import Tokenizer
from tensorflow.keras.preprocessing.sequence import pad_sequences
from sklearn.model_selection import train_test_split

# Load and preprocess your labeled dataset
# Replace 'reviews.csv' with the path to your dataset
import pandas as pd
df = pd.read_csv('reviews.csv')

# Assuming your dataset has 'text' column for reviews and 'label' column for sentiment (0 or 1)
texts = df['text']
labels = df['label']

# Tokenize the text data
tokenizer = Tokenizer(num_words=10000)  # You can adjust the vocabulary size
tokenizer.fit_on_texts(texts)
sequences = tokenizer.texts_to_sequences(texts)

# Pad the sequences to ensure uniform length
sequences = pad_sequences(sequences, maxlen=100)  # You can adjust the sequence length

# Split the data into training and validation sets
X_train, X_val, y_train, y_val = train_test_split(sequences, labels, test_size=0.2, random_state=42)

# Build an RNN model (LSTM) for sentiment analysis
model = keras.Sequential([
    keras.layers.Embedding(10000, 16, input_length=100),
    keras.layers.LSTM(64),
    keras.layers.Dense(1, activation='sigmoid')
])

model.compile(optimizer='adam', loss='binary_crossentropy', metrics=['accuracy'])
```

```
# Train the model
model.fit(X_train, y_train, epochs=5, batch_size=32)  # Adjust the number of epochs and batch size

# Evaluate the model on the validation set
val_loss, val_accuracy = model.evaluate(X_val, y_val)
print(f'Validation loss: {val_loss:.4f}, Validation accuracy: {val_accuracy:.4f}')

# Make predictions on new reviews
new_reviews = ["This product is amazing!", "Waste of money."]
new_sequences = tokenizer.texts_to_sequences(new_reviews)
new_sequences = pad_sequences(new_sequences, maxlen=100)
predictions = model.predict(new_sequences)

# Interpret the predictions for sentiment (0 for negative, 1 for positive)
for i, review in enumerate(new_reviews):
    sentiment = "Positive" if predictions[i] > 0.5 else "Negative"
    print(f"Review: {review} => Sentiment: {sentiment}")
```

In this code:

- We load your dataset of reviews (assuming it's in a CSV file) and preprocess it, including tokenization and padding.
- We create a simple LSTMbased RNN model for sentiment analysis and compile it.
- We train the model on your preprocessed training data and evaluate it on the validation set.
- Finally, we make predictions on new reviews and interpret the sentiment based on the model's predictions.

You may need to adjust hyper parameters, such as the vocabulary size, sequence length, and model architecture, to better fit your specific dataset and requirements. Additionally, if your dataset is not in a CSV format, you'll need to adapt the data loading and preprocessing steps accordingly.

Exercise: Chapter 1 & 2:

Long Questions:

Question 1: What is deep learning, and how does it differ from traditional machine learning?

Answer:
Deep learning is a subfield of machine learning that focuses on artificial neural networks, particularly deep neural networks with many layers (hence the term "deep"). It differs from traditional machine learning in the following ways:

Depth: Deep learning models have multiple hidden layers, allowing them to learn hierarchical representations of data, while traditional machine learning models often have fewer layers.

Feature Engineering: Deep learning automates feature extraction from raw data, reducing the need for manual feature engineering, which is prevalent in traditional machine learning.

Representation Learning: Deep learning models learn to extract and transform data into meaningful representations, enabling them to discover complex patterns and relationships.

Scale: Deep learning models require large datasets and significant computational resources, making them suitable for big data applications.

Question 2: What are neural networks, and how do they function in deep learning?

Answer:
Neural networks are the fundamental building blocks of deep learning. They are inspired by the structure and function of biological neurons. A neural network consists of layers, including an input layer, one or more hidden layers, and an output layer. Each neuron (or node) in a layer is connected to neurons in the adjacent layers. Neural networks function by:

- Receiving input data through the input layer.
- Propagating the data through the network, performing weighted summations and applying activation functions.
- Learning to adjust the weights during training to minimize the difference between predicted and actual outputs (back propagation).
- Generating predictions or classifications through the output layer. Neural networks can perform various tasks, including regression, classification, and more.

Question 3: What is the history and evolution of neural networks and deep learning?

Answer:
The history of neural networks and deep learning is marked by several key milestones:

1943: McCulloch and Pitts introduced the first mathematical model of a simplified neuron.

1957: Rosenblatt developed the perceptron, an early form of neural network.

1980s: Neural networks faced limitations, and research waned in favor of rulebased AI.

Late 1990s: Support vector machines gained prominence in machine learning.

2010s: Deep learning experienced a revival, fueled by the availability of large datasets and increased computational power.

Key Developments: Breakthroughs include convolutional neural networks (CNNs) for image recognition, recurrent neural networks (RNNs) for sequential data, and transformer models like BERT and GPT for natural language processing.

Question 4: What are the major applications of deep learning in today's world?

Answer:
Deep learning has found applications across various domains, including:

Computer Vision: Deep learning powers image and video analysis, enabling facial recognition, object detection, and autonomous vehicles.

Natural Language Processing: It underpins language understanding, machine translation, sentiment analysis, and chatbots.

Healthcare: Deep learning aids medical image analysis, disease diagnosis, drug discovery, and personalized treatment.

Finance: It supports fraud detection, risk assessment, and algorithmic trading.

Recommender Systems: Deep learning enhances product recommendations in ecommerce and content recommendations in streaming platforms.

Autonomous Systems: Deep learning is crucial for autonomous robots, drones, and selfdriving cars.

Question 5: What are some challenges and limitations of deep learning?

Answer:
While powerful, deep learning faces several challenges and limitations, including:

Data Requirements: Deep learning models demand substantial labeled data for training, limiting their applicability to domains with data scarcity.

Computation Resources: Training deep neural networks requires significant computational resources, including GPUs or TPUs.

Over-fitting: Deep models can easily overfit to training data, necessitating careful regularization techniques.

Interpretability: Deep learning models often lack transparency and are considered "black boxes," making it challenging to explain their decisions.

High Dimensionality: Deep models struggle with high dimensional data, requiring dimensionality reduction techniques.

Ethical Concerns: The use of deep learning in sensitive applications raises ethical issues, including bias and privacy concerns.

These answers provide a comprehensive overview of deep learning, its applications, history, and associated challenges.

Short Questions:

Question 1: What is deep learning?
Answer: Deep learning is a subfield of machine learning that focuses on neural networks with many layers, allowing the model to learn hierarchical representations of data.

Question 2: How does deep learning differ from traditional machine learning?
Answer: Deep learning models have multiple layers, automating feature extraction and enabling them to discover complex patterns, while traditional machine learning models often require manual feature engineering.

Question 3: What is a neural network in deep learning?
Answer: A neural network is the fundamental building block of deep learning, consisting of layers of interconnected neurons that process data and learn to make predictions.

Question 4: What role do activation functions play in neural networks?
Answer: Activation functions introduce nonlinearity to neural network models, enabling them to learn complex relationships in data.

Question 5: How do deep learning models adjust their weights during training?
Answer: Deep learning models use back propagation to iteratively adjust the weights to minimize the difference between predicted and actual outputs.

Question 6: What are the major applications of deep learning in computer vision?
Answer: Deep learning is used in computer vision for tasks like image classification, object detection, facial recognition, and autonomous driving.

Question 7: In what ways is deep learning applied in natural language processing (NLP)?
Answer: Deep learning is applied in NLP for tasks like machine translation, sentiment analysis, named entity recognition, and chatbots.

Question 8: What historical developments led to the resurgence of deep learning in the 2010s?
Answer: Key developments included the availability of large datasets, increased computational power, and breakthroughs in deep learning architectures like CNNs and RNNs.

Question 9: What are the challenges of training deep learning models?
Answer: Challenges include the need for substantial labeled data, computational resources, addressing over-fitting, and model interpretability.

Question 10: What ethical concerns are associated with the use of deep learning in AI applications?
Answer: Ethical concerns include issues related to bias in models, privacy violations, and the social impact of AI technologies.

Numerical Problems

Problem 1: Calculate the output of a simple feedforward neural network with one hidden layer. The input layer has 3 neurons, the hidden layer has 4 neurons, and the output layer has 2 neurons. The activation function is a sigmoid function.

Solution:

To calculate the output, you'll need the weights and biases for each layer and apply the sigmoid activation function. The specific values depend on the model.

Problem 2: Find the derivative of the sigmoid activation function, $\sigma(x)$, with respect to x.

Solution:

The derivative of the sigmoid function $\sigma(x)$ is $\sigma(x)$ $(1$ $\sigma(x))$.

Problem 3: Given a neural network with back propagation, calculate the weight updates for a single training example using the stochastic gradient descent (SGD) algorithm.

Solution:

You'll need to apply the chain rule to calculate the weight updates. The specific values depend on the network and the training example.

Problem 4:

For a binary classification problem, calculate the cross entropy loss for a predicted probability of 0.7 and the true label of 1.

Solution:

The cross entropy loss is calculated as $[y$ $\log(p) + (1$ $y)$ $\log(1$ $p)]$, where y is the true label (1 in this case) and p is the predicted probability (0.7 in this case).

Problem 5: Given a convolutional neural network (CNN) with a 3x3 filter and a 5x5 input image, calculate the output size of the feature map and the number of parameters in the convolutional layer.

Solution:

The output size of the feature map can be calculated as $(N$ $F + 2P) / S + 1$, where N is the input size, F is the filter size, P is the padding, and S is the stride. The number of parameters is equal to the filter size plus one for the bias.

Problem 6: Find the solution to a system of linear equations involving matrix multiplication. For example, solve the system $Ax = b$, where A is a 3x3 matrix, x is a 3x1 vector, and b is a 3x1 vector.

Solution:

You can use matrix algebra to find the solution $x = A^{-1} b$, where A^{-1} is the inverse of matrix A.

Problem 8: Calculate the gradient of the ReLU activation function, $f(x) = \max(0, x)$, with respect to x.

Solution:

The gradient of the ReLU function is 1 for $x > 0$ and 0 for $x < 0$.

Problem 9: Find the Eigen values and eigenvectors of a given square matrix A.

Solution:

You can use numerical techniques or software (e.g., Python's NumPy) to find the Eigen values and eigenvectors of matrix A.

Problem 10: Calculate the mean squared error (MSE) loss between a set of predicted values and the corresponding true values.

Solution:

The MSE is calculated as the mean of the squared differences between predicted and true values. For N data points, it's $(1/N) \Sigma(y\_pred \ y\_true)^2$.

Note that the specific values and matrices may vary for these problems based on the context of the deep learning model.

Chapter 3: Transfer Learning

3.1 Introduction

In the field of deep learning, one of the most powerful techniques that has gained prominence in recent years is "transfer learning." Transfer learning leverages the knowledge gained from training a neural network on one task and applies it to a different, but related, task. This approach has become invaluable in various domains, including computer vision, natural language processing, and more.

In this chapter, we will delve into the concept of transfer learning, its significance, and its applications. We will explore how transfer learning can save time and computational resources, improve model performance, and facilitate the development of deep learning solutions in real-world scenarios.

3.1.1 The Paradigm Shift

In traditional machine learning, models are typically trained from scratch for each specific task. This approach often requires extensive datasets and computational resources, making it impractical for many real-world applications. Moreover, training deep neural networks from the ground up can be time-consuming and may not yield satisfactory results when labeled data is scarce.

Transfer learning represents a paradigm shift in the world of deep learning. Instead of starting with a blank slate, it allows us to harness the knowledge embedded in pre-trained models and adapt them for new tasks. This approach has proven to be highly effective, especially when dealing with limited data.

The Core Idea

At the heart of transfer learning is the idea that features learned by a neural network for one task can be useful for another task. Imagine training a model to recognize thousands of objects in images. The knowledge acquired by this model about object shapes, textures, and patterns can be invaluable when developing an image classifier for a specific category of objects, like cats and dogs. This is where transfer learning steps in.

Types of Transfer Learning

Transfer learning can be categorized into several types, each suited to different scenarios:

1. Feature Extraction: In this approach, we take a pre-trained model and remove its final classification layer. The remaining layers serve as feature extractors. New classification layers are then added, and the model is fine-tuned on the target task. Feature extraction is particularly useful when the source and target tasks share low-level features.

2. Fine-Tuning: Fine-tuning extends feature extraction. Here, we not only remove the final layer but also adjust some of the earlier layers. By allowing a portion of the network to adapt to the new task, fine-tuning can be highly effective when the source and target tasks share some high-level features.

3. Domain Adaptation: Domain adaptation is used when the source and target tasks come from different domains, where the data distributions may vary significantly. Techniques like adversarial training and domain-specific layers help the model adapt to the new domain.

Benefits of Transfer Learning

The advantages of transfer learning are manifold:

- Improved Model Performance: Transfer learning can lead to better and faster convergence, especially when working with limited data. It allows models to generalize well on new tasks.
- Reduced Data Requirements: Instead of requiring large volumes of labeled data for each new task, transfer learning leverages the knowledge from a broad range of pre-trained models.
- Time and Resource Efficiency: Training deep neural networks is computationally expensive. Transfer learning, in many cases, reduces the training time and resource requirements by using pre-trained models as a starting point.
- Real-World Applicability: In practice, it's often challenging to collect extensive labeled data for every specific task. Transfer learning facilitates the rapid development and deployment of deep learning models in real-world applications.

Transfer learning has emerged as a game-changer in the field of deep learning, offering a way to overcome challenges related to data scarcity, computational resources, and time constraints. In the following sections of this chapter, we will explore the mechanics of transfer learning, the different strategies, and practical examples of its application in various domains.

Transfer learning is a machine learning technique where a model developed for one task is reused as the starting point for a model on a second task. This can be done when the two tasks are related, and the knowledge learned for the first task can be applied to the second task.

Transfer learning is a powerful technique that can be used to improve the performance of machine learning models on a wide variety of tasks. It can also be used to reduce the amount of data and computing resources required to train a model.

Applications of Transfer Learning

Transfer learning can be used for a wide variety of tasks, including:

- Image Classification: Transfer learning is widely used for image classification tasks. Pre-trained models like VGG, ResNet, and Inception have been adapted for specific image classification tasks, such as identifying different plant species, detecting diseases in medical images, or classifying satellite images.
- NLP and Language Understanding: In natural language processing, pre-trained language models like BERT and GPT-3 have revolutionized tasks such as sentiment analysis, text classification, and machine translation. Fine-tuning these models on domain-specific text data can yield state-of-the-art results.
- Object Detection: Transfer learning can be applied to object detection tasks. Models pre-trained on large image datasets can be fine-tuned for detecting specific objects in images or videos.
- Recommendation Systems: In recommendation systems, transfer learning can be used to understand user behavior from historical data and provide personalized recommendations, even when the user has limited interaction with the platform.

Challenges of Transfer Learning

There are a number of challenges associated with using transfer learning, including:

- Domain mismatch: The two tasks need to be related in order for transfer learning to be effective. If the two tasks are too different, then the knowledge learned for the first task may not be transferable to the second task.

- Negative transfer: In some cases, transfer learning can lead to negative transfer, where the knowledge learned for the first task actually harms the performance of the model on the second task.

- Model adaptation: It is often necessary to adapt the pre-trained model to the new task. This can be done by fine-tuning the model's parameters on the new task's training data.

Future of Transfer Learning

Transfer learning is a rapidly evolving field, and new advances are being made all the time. One of the most promising areas of research in transfer learning is the development of methods for adapting pre-trained models to new tasks without the need for fine-tuning. This would make transfer learning even more accessible and efficient.

Another promising area of research is the development of methods for transfer learning between tasks that are very different from each other. This would allow researchers to apply the knowledge learned from one task to a wide range of other tasks.

Overall, transfer learning is a powerful technique with a bright future. As research in this area continues, we can expect to see transfer learning used in even more ways to solve real-world problems.

Examples of Transfer Learning in Use

Here are a few examples of how transfer learning is being used in the real world today:

- Google Translate: Google Translate uses transfer learning to translate text between over 100 languages.

- Facebook Photos: Facebook Photos uses transfer learning to identify people and objects in photos.

- Amazon Alexa: Amazon Alexa uses transfer learning to understand and respond to voice commands.

- Tesla Autopilot: Tesla Autopilot uses transfer learning to identify objects on the road and make decisions about how to drive the car.

- Medical diagnosis: Transfer learning is being used to develop models that can diagnose diseases and predict patient outcomes, such as the risk of developing cancer

3.1.2 Transfer Learning Mechanics

How Transfer Learning Works?

Transfer learning operates under the assumption that features extracted by a neural network's layers are hierarchical, with lower layers detecting low-level features like edges and textures, and higher layers capturing more abstract information. These learned features can be considered as representations of the input data that are progressively more abstract and task-agnostic as you move up the network.

When transferring knowledge from one task to another, you typically take a pre-trained model, remove its final classification layer, and add a new layer tailored to your specific task. The feature extractors in the pre-trained model are fine-tuned to better align with the new task. This fine-tuning process helps the model learn the most relevant high-level features.

Choosing a Pre-Trained Model

Selecting an appropriate pre-trained model for your transfer learning task is crucial. The choice of the pre-trained model depends on the nature of your data and the similarity between the source and target tasks. For instance:

- If you are working with image data, models pre-trained on the ImageNet dataset, such as VGG16, ResNet, and Inception, are often good starting points for various image classification tasks.
- If your task involves natural language processing (NLP), pre-trained models like BERT, GPT, or RoBERTa are commonly used.

Strategies for Transfer Learning

Transfer learning encompasses a variety of strategies that cater to different use cases. Here are some of the most common ones:

Feature Extraction

In feature extraction, the pre-trained model is used as a fixed feature extractor. Its lower and middle layers are frozen, ensuring that they retain their learned features. Only the final layers, responsible for the specific classification task, are modified and fine-tuned for the target task.

Feature extraction is ideal when the source and target tasks share low-level features. For example, the convolutional layers of a pre-trained image classification model can be highly effective at capturing general image features that are relevant to a specific classification task.

Fine-Tuning

Fine-tuning takes feature extraction a step further by allowing the adjustment of some of the earlier layers in addition to the final layers. This strategy is particularly beneficial when the source and target tasks share both low and high-level features. In fine-tuning, you can fine-tune a portion of the pre-trained model while keeping some layers frozen. For instance, you might keep the lower layers frozen (representing low-level features) and fine-tune only the middle and top layers, which capture high-level abstractions.

Domain Adaptation

Domain adaptation is a strategy used when the source and target tasks belong to different data domains. In such cases, the data distributions may differ significantly. Techniques like adversarial training and domain-specific layers are employed to help the model adapt to the new domain.

For example, if you have a model trained on medical images and you want to adapt it to images from a different hospital with slightly different characteristics, domain adaptation techniques can help bridge the domain gap.

In the upcoming sections of this chapter, we will explore these practical applications in detail, providing hands-on examples and insights into how transfer learning can be effectively utilized in different contexts. We will also delve into the technical implementation, including code snippets, best practices, and common challenges that you might encounter when applying transfer learning.

3.3 Hands-on Transfer Learning

In this section, we'll dive into hands-on examples of transfer learning across various domains. We'll provide practical code snippets and guidance to help you understand the process better and apply it to your specific use cases.

- Image Classification
- Using Pre-Trained Models for Image Classification

In image classification, transfer learning is often used to create powerful image classifiers for specific tasks. The key idea is to use a pre-trained model and fine-tune it on your own image dataset. This approach not only saves you time but also leverages the general features learned by the pre-trained model. Let's walk through a simplified example using TensorFlow and Keras:

```
import tensorflow as tf
from tensorflow import keras
from tensorflow.keras.applications import VGG16
from tensorflow.keras.layers import Dense, GlobalAveragePooling2D
from tensorflow.keras.models import Model
from tensorflow.keras.optimizers import Adam
from sklearn.model_selection import train_test_split
import numpy as np
# Load your image dataset and preprocess it
# Create a base model using a pre-trained VGG16 model
base_model = VGG16(weights='imagenet', include_top=False)
# Add custom classification layers on top of the base model
x = base_model.output
x = GlobalAveragePooling2D()(x)
x = Dense(1024, activation='relu')(x)
```

```
predictions = Dense(num_classes, activation='softmax')(x)
# Create the new model
model = Model(inputs=base_model.input, outputs=predictions)
# Freeze the layers of the pre-trained model
for layer in base_model.layers:
    layer.trainable = False
# Compile the model
model.compile(optimizer=Adam(lr=0.0001), loss='categorical_crossentropy', metrics=['accuracy'])
# Split the data into training and validation sets
X_train, X_val, y_train, y_val = train_test_split(X, y, test_size=0.2, random_state=42)
# Train the model
model.fit(X_train, y_train, epochs=10, batch_size=32)
# Evaluate the model
val_loss, val_acc = model.evaluate(X_val, y_val)
print(f'Validation loss: {val_loss:.4f}, Validation accuracy: {val_acc:.4f}')
```

This code shows how to build an image classifier using a pre-trained VGG16 model and fine-tuning it for your specific classification task.

- Natural Language Processing (NLP)
- Fine-Tuning Pre-Trained Language Models

In natural language processing, pre-trained language models such as BERT, GPT-3, and RoBERTa have revolutionized various NLP tasks. Here's a simplified example of fine-tuning a pre-trained BERT model for sentiment analysis using the Hugging Face Transformers library:

```
from transformers import BertTokenizer, BertForSequenceClassification, Trainer, TrainingArguments
from sklearn.model_selection import train_test_split
# Load and preprocess your text dataset
# Initialize a pre-trained BERT model and tokenizer
model_name = 'bert-base-uncased'
tokenizer = BertTokenizer.from_pre-trained(model_name)
model = BertForSequenceClassification.from_pre-trained(model_name)
# Tokenize and format the data
encoded_data_train = tokenizer(texts, truncation=True, padding=True)
encoded_data_val = tokenizer(val_texts, truncation=True, padding=True)
# Split the data into training and validation sets
X_train, X_val, y_train, y_val = train_test_split(encoded_data_train, labels, test_size=0.2, random_state=42)
# Fine-tune the BERT model
training_args = TrainingArguments(
    per_device_train_batch_size=32,
```

```
    evaluation_strategy='steps',
    eval_steps=500,
    save_total_limit=1,
)
trainer = Trainer(
    model=model,
    args=training_args,
    train_dataset=X_train,
    eval_dataset=X_val,
)
trainer.train()
# Evaluate the model
results = trainer.evaluate()
print(results)
```

This code demonstrates how to fine-tune a pre-trained BERT model for sentiment analysis on your specific text data.

```
# Object Detection
# Transfer Learning for Object Detection
```

Transfer learning is also applicable to object detection tasks. You can leverage pre-trained models like Faster R-CNN or YOLO (You Only Look Once) and fine-tune them for your specific object detection task. Here's a simplified example using TensorFlow and the TensorFlow Object Detection API:

```
import tensorflow as tf
from object_detection.utils import config_util
from object_detection.builders import model_builder
from object_detection.utils import visualization_utils as viz_utils
from object_detection.utils import config_util


# Load and preprocess your object detection dataset
# Load pre-trained Faster R-CNN model
MODEL_DIR        =        'pre-trained_models/faster_rcnn_inception_resnet_v2_1024x1024_coco17_tpu-
8/saved_model'
detect_fn = tf.saved_model.load(MODEL_DIR)
# Convert label map to category index
category_index        =        label_map_util.create_category_index_from_labelmap(PATH_TO_LABELS,
use_display_name=True)
# Split the data into training and validation sets
X_train, X_val = train_test_split(X, test_size=0.2, random_state=42)
# Fine-tune the Faster R-CNN model
for image, label in X_train:
    input_tensor = tf.convert_to_tensor(image)
    detections = detect_fn(input_tensor)
```

```
# Process detections as needed
```

3.7 State of the art pre-trained models

3.7.1 Computer Vision Models:

1. VGG (Visual Geometry Group): VGG models are known for their simplicity and effectiveness. Variants such as VGG16 and VGG19 were widely used for image classification.

2. ResNet (Residual Network): ResNet introduced the concept of residual connections, allowing the training of very deep neural networks. Variants like ResNet-50 and ResNet-101 achieved impressive accuracy on image classification tasks.

3. Inception (GoogLeNet): Inception models, including InceptionV3 and Inception-ResNet, are known for their utilization of "inception" modules, which enable efficient training and high accuracy.

4. Xception: An extension of the Inception concept, Xception focuses on depth-wise separable convolutions, reducing the number of parameters while maintaining accuracy.

5. EfficientNet: EfficientNet models optimize the trade-off between model size and accuracy by scaling model depth, width, and resolution. They are efficient and highly accurate.

6. DenseNet: DenseNet is based on the idea of densely connected layers. Each layer is connected to every other layer in a feed forward fashion. It achieves excellent results while being computationally efficient.

7. YOLO (You Only Look Once): YOLO is a real-time object detection model that has gone through several versions, with YOLOv4 being one of the most advanced at the time. It's known for its speed and accuracy in real-time object detection.

8. Faster R-CNN: Faster R-CNN is a widely used model for object detection. It combines deep learning with region proposal networks (RPNs) to achieve high accuracy.

3.7.2 Natural Language Processing (NLP) Models:

1. BERT (Bidirectional Encoder Representations from Transformers): BERT is a revolutionary NLP model pre-trained on massive text corpora. It introduced the concept of bidirectional contextual embeddings, significantly advancing the state of the art in a wide range of NLP tasks, including sentiment analysis, text classification, and question-answering.

2. GPT (Generative Pre-trained Transformer): The GPT series, including GPT-2 and GPT-3, are autoregressive language models that have set new benchmarks in tasks like text generation, machine translation, and language understanding.

3. XLNet: XLNet, based on the Transformer architecture, extends BERT by allowing permutations of input sequences. It achieved state-of-the-art performance in various NLP benchmarks.

4. RoBERTa: RoBERTa is a model built on BERT's architecture with further optimization. It employs large-scale pre-training and outperforms BERT on several NLP benchmarks.

5. T5 (Text-to-Text Transfer Transformer): T5 treats all NLP tasks as text-to-text tasks, making it a versatile model for a wide range of NLP tasks. It achieved strong results across different benchmarks.

6. ERNIE (Enhanced Representation through kNowledge IntEgration): ERNIE, developed by Baidu, incorporates knowledge from structured data sources to enhance its understanding of language, making it effective for tasks requiring world knowledge.

7. ALBERT (A Lite BERT): ALBERT focuses on reducing the number of parameters in the model while maintaining performance. It achieves similar accuracy to BERT with significantly fewer parameters.

8. ELECTRA: ELECTRA introduces a new pre-training task called "replaced token detection," which enables more efficient training and impressive results in NLP tasks.

9. Turing-NLG: OpenAI's Turing-NLG is a powerful and versatile language model. It can be fine-tuned for various NLP tasks, including text generation and language understanding.

These state-of-the-art pre-trained models have significantly advanced the fields of computer vision and natural language processing. Their availability and ease of fine-tuning have democratized the development of deep learning solutions in these domains. It's essential to consider the specific requirements of your task and the availability of pre-trained models when choosing the right one for your project.

Exercise Chapter 3:

Question 1: What is transfer learning, and how does it work in the context of deep learning models? Provide an in-depth explanation of the different transfer learning scenarios and their applications.

Answer:

Transfer learning is a technique in machine learning where knowledge gained from one task (the source task) is applied to another related task (the target task). In deep learning, it's often used with pre-trained neural networks. There are several transfer learning scenarios:

1. Feature Extraction: In this scenario, you use the pre-trained model's layers as a feature extractor. You remove the final layers and append new layers specific to your target task. The lower layers capture generic features like edges and textures, while the higher layers learn more task-specific features.

2. Fine-tuning: Fine-tuning extends feature extraction. You not only add new layers but also update the weights of the pre-trained layers. This allows the network to adapt to your specific task.

3. Domain Adaptation: Domain adaptation is used when the source and target domains are somewhat different. It aims to adapt the model to the differences between the two domains while preserving the knowledge from the source domain.

4. Lifelong/Sequential Learning: This scenario involves continuous learning on a series of tasks, where knowledge from previous tasks is retained and applied to new tasks. Elastic Weight Consolidation (EWC) is a technique used to mitigate catastrophic forgetting in this scenario.

Applications of transfer learning are extensive, including image classification, object detection, sentiment analysis, and language translation. It's particularly valuable when you have a small target dataset, as it leverages the knowledge encoded in pre-trained models.

Question 2: Explain the concept of model selection and adaptation in the context of transfer learning. How can you choose the most suitable pre-trained model for your target task, and what adaptations may be needed?

Answer: Model selection and adaptation are crucial steps in transfer learning. To select the most suitable pre-trained model, you should consider the following factors:

- Similarity to Target Task: Choose a pre-trained model that was trained on a source task that is similar to your target task in terms of data and features. For example, if you're working on an image classification task for medical images, a pre-trained model on general object recognition may not be as effective as a model trained on medical images.
- Model Size: Smaller models may be preferred when you have limited computational resources, whereas larger models may offer better performance if resources are not a concern.
- Architecture: The architecture of the pre-trained model should align with your target task. For example, convolutional neural networks (CNNs) are a natural choice for image-related tasks.

Adaptation involves:

- Replacing the Classifier: In many cases, you need to remove the final classification layers of the pre-trained model and add new layers tailored to your target task. The architecture of these layers should match the requirements of your task.
- Fine-Tuning: Depending on your target dataset's size and the similarity between the source and target tasks, you may need to fine-tune the pre-trained model's layers, allowing them to learn task-specific features. However, fine-tuning should be carefully controlled to avoid over-fitting.

Choosing the right pre-trained model and adapting it effectively can significantly impact the success of your transfer learning application.

Question 3: Discuss the challenges and strategies associated with domain adaptation in transfer learning. Provide examples of domain adaptation problems and how they are addressed.

Answer: Domain adaptation is a subfield of transfer learning that deals with adapting a model trained on a source domain to a different but related target domain. Challenges in domain adaptation include domain shift, limited target data, and the risk of over-fitting to the source domain.

Strategies for domain adaptation include:
- Feature-Level Adaptation: This involves mapping the source domain data and target domain data to a common feature space. One method is Principal Component Analysis (PCA)-based adaptation.

- Instance-Level Adaptation: You can weight the importance of instances from the source domain differently to reduce the impact of the source domain's biases.
- Model-Level Adaptation: This includes fine-tuning specific layers or adapting the model's architecture to suit the target domain.

Examples of domain adaptation problems include:
- Adaptation for Cross-Domain Sentiment Analysis: When you train a sentiment analysis model on reviews from one domain (e.g., movies) and want to apply it to another domain (e.g., books).
- Cross-Domain Object Detection: Adapting object detection models trained on one set of images to another with different properties, like style and lighting conditions.
- Domain Adaptation in Medical Imaging: Adapting a model trained on images from one hospital to another with variations in equipment or patient demographics.

These problems often involve domain-specific biases and variations that must be mitigated to ensure the model's effectiveness.

Question 4: Explain the concept of catastrophic forgetting and its relevance to transfer learning, lifelong learning, and sequential learning in deep neural networks. How can techniques like Elastic Weight Consolidation (EWC) address this challenge?

Answer: Catastrophic forgetting occurs when a neural network forgets previously learned information when adapting to new tasks. It's a significant challenge in transfer learning, lifelong learning, and sequential learning scenarios.

In lifelong or sequential learning, when a model is trained on multiple tasks, the network's weights are updated to fit the current task, often causing the loss of knowledge related to previously learned tasks. To mitigate catastrophic forgetting, techniques like Elastic Weight Consolidation (EWC) are used. EWC works as follows:

1. Task Importance: EWC quantifies the importance of each parameter in relation to previously learned tasks. Parameters that are important for past tasks receive higher weights.

2. Regularization: During training on a new task, EWC introduces regularization terms that discourage significant changes.

Chapter 4: Reinforcement Learning

4.1 Introduction

Reinforcement Learning (RL) is a subfield of machine learning that focuses on training agents to make sequences of decisions in an environment to maximize a cumulative reward. Unlike supervised learning, where the model is provided with labeled data, or unsupervised learning, where the model discovers patterns in data without explicit guidance, reinforcement learning agents learn through interaction with an environment.

RL is inspired by behavioral psychology and has found success in various applications, such as game playing, robotics, recommendation systems, and autonomous driving. This chapter explores the fundamental concepts, algorithms, and applications of reinforcement learning.

Reinforcement learning (RL) is a type of machine learning that allows agents to learn how to behave in an environment by trial and error. RL agents are rewarded for taking actions that lead to desired outcomes and penalized for taking actions that lead to undesired outcomes. Over time, RL agents learn to take actions that maximize their rewards.

RL is a powerful technique that can be used to train agents to perform a wide variety of tasks, including:

- Playing games, such as Go and Atari games

- Controlling robots

- Managing portfolios

- Optimizing supply chains

RL agents can learn to perform these tasks without being explicitly programmed how to do them. Instead, they learn by interacting with their environment and receiving feedback.

One of the key advantages of RL is that it can be used to train agents to perform tasks in environments that are too complex or dynamic to be modeled explicitly. This makes RL a well-suited technique for training agents to perform tasks in the real world.

Challenges of Reinforcement Learning

RL is a powerful technique, but it has a few challenges. One challenge is that RL can be slow to learn. RL agents need to interact with the environment many times before they learn to perform a task well.

Another challenge is that RL agents can be sensitive to the hyper parameters of the RL algorithm. The hyper parameters are parameters that control how the RL algorithm works. It can be difficult to find the right hyper parameters for a particular task.

Finally, RL agents can be unstable. This means that they can sometimes learn to behave in unexpected ways.

RL is a powerful technique for training agents to perform a wide variety of tasks. RL is well-suited for training agents to perform tasks in environments that are too complex or dynamic to be modeled explicitly.

However, RL has a few challenges, such as slow learning, sensitivity to hyper parameters, and instability.

Despite these challenges, RL is a promising area of research with the potential to revolutionize the way that we train machines to perform tasks.

4.2 How Reinforcement Learning Works

RL agents learn by interacting with their environment and receiving feedback. At each time step, the agent takes an action and observes the next state of the environment. The agent also receives a reward, which is a scalar value that indicates how good or bad the agent's action was.

The agent's goal is to maximize its expected reward over time. To do this, the agent needs to learn which actions lead to the highest rewards in each state of the environment.

RL agents learn using a variety of algorithms. One common algorithm is Q-learning. Q-learning works by maintaining a Q-table, which is a table that maps from state-action pairs to Q-values. The Q-value for a state-action pair is the expected reward that the agent will receive if it takes that action in that state.

The agent updates the Q-values in the Q-table as it interacts with the environment. At each time step, the agent updates the Q-value for the state-action pair that it took by adding the reward that it received to the Q-value.

The agent then uses the Q-values to choose its next action. The agent chooses the action that has the highest Q-value in the current state.

Over time, the agent learns to choose actions that lead to the highest rewards in each state of the environment.

4.2.1 A Generalized Reinforcement Learning Model:

Here is a code snippet about a generalized Reinforcement Learning model.

```
graph LR
subgraph State
    subgraph Environment
        Process State
        Generate Next State
    end
    subgraph Agent
        Select Action
        Execute Action
    end
end
subgraph Reward
    Calculate Reward
end
Agent --> Reward
```

```
Reward --> State
State --> Agent
```

The flow diagram shows the following steps:

1. The agent observes the current state of the environment.

2. The agent selects an action to take.

3. The agent takes the action in the environment.

4. The environment transitions to the next state and generates a reward for the agent.

5. The agent receives the reward and updates its policy.

The agent's policy is a function that maps from states to actions. The agent updates its policy to try to maximize its expected reward over time.

The agent can learn to perform tasks by interacting with the environment and receiving rewards. Over time, the agent will learn to choose actions that lead to the highest rewards.

This is a generalized reinforcement learning model. It can be used to train agents to perform a wide variety of tasks, including playing games, controlling robots, managing portfolios, and optimizing supply chains.

Here is an example of how the generalized reinforcement learning model could be used to train an agent to play a game:

1. The agent observes the current state of the game board.

2. The agent selects a move to make.

3. The agent makes the move on the game board.

4. The game transitions to the next state and generates a reward for the agent (e.g., +1 for winning the game, -1 for losing the game).

5. The agent receives the reward and updates its policy.

Over time, the agent will learn to make moves that lead to winning the game.

4.2.2 Key Components of Reinforcement Learning

Reinforcement learning systems consist of three key components:

Agent

The agent is the decision-maker in the RL system. It takes actions in the environment based on its observations and the information it has learned through experience. The agent's objective is to maximize its cumulative reward over time.

Environment

The environment is the external system with which the agent interacts. It provides feedback to the agent in the form of rewards, which the agent seeks to maximize. The environment can be anything from a virtual world in a computer program to the real world in robotics applications.

Reward

The reward is a numerical value that the agent receives from the environment after taking an action. It indicates the immediate benefit or cost of that action. The agent's goal is to learn a policy (a strategy) that maximizes the expected cumulative reward.

4.2.3 Markov Decision Process (MDP)

A Markov Decision Process (MDP) is a mathematical framework for modeling sequential decision-making problems under uncertainty. It is a powerful tool for reinforcement learning (RL), which is a type of machine learning that allows agents to learn how to behave in an environment by trial and error.

An MDP is defined by the following components:

- A set of states, S

- A set of actions, A

- A transition function, T, which maps from state-action pairs to probability distributions over next states

- A reward function, R, which maps from state-action pairs to rewards

At each time step, the agent is in a state s and can take an action a. The agent then transitions to a new state s' with probability T(s', s, a). The agent also receives a reward R(s, a).

The agent's goal is to maximize its expected reward over time. To do this, the agent needs to learn which actions lead to the highest rewards in each state of the environment.

MDPs are well-suited for modeling a wide variety of RL problems, such as:

- Playing games

- Controlling robots

- Managing portfolios

- Optimizing supply chains

For example, an MDP could be used to model the game of Go. The states of the MDP would be the positions of the stones on the Go board. The actions of the MDP would be the moves that the agent can make. The transition function would map from state-action pairs to probability distributions over next states. The reward function would reward the agent for winning the game and penalize the agent for losing the game.

MDPs can be used to solve RL problems using a variety of algorithms, such as Q-learning, policy gradients, and value iteration. These algorithms typically work by iteratively updating the agent's policy. At each step, the agent updates its policy to try to maximize its expected reward over time.

MDPs are a powerful tool for RL. They provide a formal framework for modeling sequential decision-making problems under uncertainty. MDPs can be used to solve a wide variety of RL problems using a variety of algorithms.

Here are some of the benefits of using MDPs for RL:

- MDPs provide a formal framework for modeling sequential decision-making problems under uncertainty. This makes it easier to understand and analyze RL problems.

- MDPs can be used to solve a wide variety of RL problems. This makes them a versatile tool for RL.

- MDPs can be used with a variety of RL algorithms. This makes it possible to choose the right algorithm for the specific problem that is being solved.

However, there are also some challenges associated with using MDPs for RL:

- MDPs can be complex to model. This is especially true for problems with a large number of states and actions.

- MDPs can be difficult to solve. This is especially true for problems with a large number of states and actions.

- MDPs can be sensitive to the hyper parameters of the RL algorithm. The hyper parameters are parameters that control how the RL algorithm works. It can be difficult to find the right hyper parameters for a particular problem.

Despite these challenges, MDPs are a powerful tool for RL. They are used to solve a wide variety of RL problems in a variety of domains.

How Real world Problems are solved using MDP
Let's take the example of a robot that is trying to navigate a maze. The goal of the robot is to reach the exit of the maze in as few steps as possible.

We can model this problem as an MDP as follows:

- States: The states of the MDP are the different locations that the robot can be in the maze.

- Actions: The actions of the MDP are the different directions that the robot can move.

- Transition function: The transition function maps from state-action pairs to probability distributions over next states. For example, if the robot is in the center of the maze and it moves north, it is 80% likely to end up in the north cell of the maze and 20% likely to end up in the west cell of the maze.

- Reward function: The reward function rewards the robot for reaching the exit of the maze and penalizes the robot for taking steps.

The robot can then use an MDP algorithm, such as Q-learning, to learn how to navigate the maze optimally.

Here is a step-by-step explanation of how the robot would use Q-learning to learn how to navigate the maze:

1. The robot initializes the Q-table. The Q-table is a table that maps from state-action pairs to Q-values. The Q-value for a state-action pair is the expected reward that the robot will receive if it takes that action in that state.

2. The robot starts in the center of the maze.

3. The robot selects an action to take. The robot can use a variety of strategies to select an action, such as epsilon-greedy exploration.

4. The robot takes the action in the environment.

5. The robot observes the next state of the environment.

6. The robot receives a reward.

7. The robot updates the Q-table. The robot updates the Q-value for the state-action pair that it took by adding the reward that it received to the Q-value.

8. The robot repeats steps 3-7 until it reaches the exit of the maze.

Over time, the robot will learn to choose actions that lead to the highest rewards in each state of the maze. This means that the robot will learn to navigate the maze optimally.

MDPs can be used to solve a wide variety of real-world problems. For example, MDPs can be used to solve problems in robotics, finance, and manufacturing.

Here are some other examples of how MDPs can be used to solve real-world problems:

- Robotics: MDPs can be used to control robots in a variety of environments, such as factories and warehouses.

- Finance: MDPs can be used to develop trading strategies and to manage portfolios.

- Manufacturing: MDPs can be used to optimize production schedules and to reduce costs.

MDPs are a powerful tool for solving sequential decision-making problems under uncertainty. They are used in a variety of domains to solve a wide variety of real-world problems.

4.3 Exploration vs. Exploitation

One of the key challenges in RL is the exploration-exploitation trade-off. The agent must balance between exploring new actions to discover potentially better policies and exploiting its current knowledge to maximize immediate rewards. Various algorithms address this trade-off.

Exploration vs. exploitation is a fundamental dilemma in machine learning, especially in reinforcement learning (RL). It is the trade-off between learning new things and using the knowledge that you already have.

Exploration is the process of trying new things to learn more about the environment and the potential rewards that are available. This can involve taking actions that are not immediately optimal, but which could lead to better rewards in the long run.

Exploitation is the process of using the knowledge that you already have to maximize your immediate rewards. This involves taking actions that are known to be good, even if they may not be the best possible actions in the long run.

The exploration-exploitation dilemma is a challenge because both exploration and exploitation are important for success. If you only explore, you will never learn how to maximize your rewards. If you only exploit, you may get stuck in a local optimum and miss out on better rewards that are available elsewhere.

The best approach to the exploration-exploitation dilemma is to balance the two. You need to explore enough to learn new things, but you also need to exploit your knowledge to maximize your immediate rewards.

There are a number of different ways to balance exploration and exploitation. One common approach is to use an epsilon-greedy policy. With an epsilon-greedy policy, the agent takes a random action with probability epsilon, and it takes the best known action with probability 1-epsilon. The value of epsilon can be adjusted to control the balance between exploration and exploitation.

Another common approach to balancing exploration and exploitation is to use a Bayesian approach. With a Bayesian approach, the agent maintains a belief distribution over the state of the environment and the potential rewards that are available. The agent then uses this belief distribution to select actions that are most likely to lead to high rewards.

The best approach to balancing exploration and exploitation will vary depending on the specific problem that is being solved. However, the exploration-exploitation dilemma is a fundamental challenge in machine learning, and it is important to be aware of the different ways to balance exploration and exploitation.

Here are some examples of the exploration-exploitation dilemma in the real world:

- A business may choose to explore new markets or products, even if this means sacrificing profits in the short term.

- A student may choose to take a difficult class to learn new things, even if this means getting a lower grade in the class.

- A gambler may choose to try their luck at a new casino, even if this means losing money in the short term.

In all of these cases, the individual or organization is trying to balance the potential rewards of exploration with the risks of exploitation.

The exploration-exploitation dilemma is a complex problem, but there are a number of different ways to balance the two. By understanding the different ways to balance exploration and exploitation, we can make better decisions in a variety of situations.

4.4 RL Algorithms

Reinforcement learning offers a variety of algorithms to solve different types of problems. Some of the most commonly used algorithms include:

Reinforcement learning (RL) is a type of machine learning that allows agents to learn how to behave in an environment by trial and error. RL agents are rewarded for taking actions that lead to desired outcomes and penalized for taking actions that lead to undesired outcomes. Over time, RL agents learn to take actions that maximize their rewards.

There are a variety of RL algorithms that can be used to solve different types of problems. Here is a brief overview of some of the most common RL algorithms:

- Q-learning: Q-learning is a simple but powerful RL algorithm. It works by maintaining a Q-table, which is a table that maps from state-action pairs to Q-values. The Q-value for a state-action pair is the expected reward that the agent will receive if it takes that action in that state. Q-learning updates the Q-values in the Q-table as it interacts with the environment. At each time step, the agent updates the Q-value for the state-action pair that it took by adding the reward that it received to the Q-value. The agent then uses the Q-values to choose its next action.

- Policy gradients: Policy gradients are a family of RL algorithms that work by directly optimizing the agent's policy. The policy is a function that maps from states to actions. Policy gradient algorithms use a variety of techniques to update the policy in order to maximize the agent's expected reward.

- Actor-critic: Actor-critic is a special type of policy gradient algorithm that uses two separate networks: an actor network and a critic network. The actor network is responsible for selecting actions, and the critic network is responsible for evaluating the actions that the actor network selects. The actor-critic algorithm updates the actor network and the critic network simultaneously in order to maximize the agent's expected reward.

- Value iteration: Value iteration is a dynamic programming algorithm that can be used to solve RL problems. Value iteration works by iteratively computing the value of each state in the environment. The value of a state is the expected reward that the agent will receive if it starts in that state and acts optimally. Once the value of each state has been computed, the agent can use this information to choose the optimal action in each state.

These are just a few of the many RL algorithms that are available. The best RL algorithm to use for a particular problem will depend on the specific characteristics of the problem.

Here are some examples of how RL algorithms can be used to solve real-world problems:

- Q-learning: Q-learning can be used to train a robot to navigate a maze. The robot can learn to navigate the maze by observing the rewards that it receives for taking different actions in different states.

- Policy gradients: Policy gradients can be used to train a stock trader to make profitable trades. The stock trader can learn to make profitable trades by observing the rewards that it receives for taking different actions in different states.

- Actor-critic: Actor-critic can be used to train a self-driving car to drive safely and efficiently. The self-driving car can learn to drive safely and efficiently by observing the rewards that it receives for taking different actions in different states.

- Value iteration: Value iteration can be used to train a manufacturing plant to optimize its production schedule. The manufacturing plant can learn to optimize its production schedule by observing the rewards that it receives for producing different products in different quantities.

RL algorithms are a powerful tool for solving a wide variety of problems. By understanding the different types of RL algorithms that are available and how they can be used, we can develop solutions to complex problems in a variety of domains.

4.5 The Grid World Example

Imagine a simple grid world, which is a 3x3 grid. The agent starts at the top-left corner and aims to reach the bottom-right corner. The agent can move in four directions: up, down, left, or right. The objective is to find the optimal policy for the agent to navigate from the start to the goal while collecting as much reward as possible.

1. States (S): In this example, the states represent the grid cells. We have a total of 9 states, each corresponding to one cell in the grid.

S = {1, 2, 3, 4, 5, 6, 7, 8, 9}

For simplicity, let's assume that the agent is currently in state 1 (top-left corner) and the goal state is state 9 (bottom-right corner).

2. Actions (A): The agent can take four possible actions: Up (U), Down (D), Left (L), or Right (R). These actions allow the agent to move within the grid.

A = {U, D, L, R}

3. State Transition Probabilities (P): The state transition probability defines the likelihood of transitioning from one state to another when taking a specific action. In our example, the transition is deterministic, meaning that the agent's action directly determines the new state.

For example, if the agent is in state 1 and takes action R (right), it will transition to state 2. The transition probability can be represented as follows:

P(1, R, 2) = 1

This equation states that if the agent is in state 1, takes action R, it is guaranteed to reach state 2.

4. Rewards (R): Each state-action pair receives a reward. The agent aims to maximize the cumulative reward over time. In our grid world example, the agent receives a negative reward (e.g., -1) for each step it takes to encourage reaching the goal quickly. The agent receives a positive reward (e.g., +10) when it reaches the goal.

R(1, R, 2) = -1 (Negative reward for moving right)

R(2, R, 3) = -1 (Negative reward for moving right)

R(8, D, 9) = +10 (Positive reward for reaching the goal)

These equations represent the reward structure in the grid world. The agent's objective is to find a policy (a strategy) that maximizes the cumulative reward over its journey.

4.6 Mathematical Representation

The mathematical representation of an RL problem involves defining the MDP components (S, A, P, R) and finding a policy (π) that guides the agent's actions to maximize the expected cumulative reward. The objective can be formulated as follows:

State-Value Function ($V\pi$): This function provides the expected cumulative reward when following policy π starting from a given state s.

$V\pi(s) = E [\sum(t=0 \text{ to } \infty) \gamma^t R(st) | s0 = s, \pi]$

Here, γ (gamma) is the discount factor, and t represents the time step.

Action-Value Function (Qπ): This function provides the expected cumulative reward when taking action a in state s and then following policy π.

Qπ(s, a) = E [$\sum$(t=0 to ∞) γ^t R(st) | s0 = s, a0 = a, π]

Optimal Policy (π): The optimal policy is the one that maximizes the expected cumulative reward. It can be found by solving for the state-value function V or the action-value function Q.

Bellman Equation: The Bellman equation relates the value of a state or state-action pair to the values of subsequent states or state-action pairs. It is a key concept in RL and is used to derive value iteration and policy iteration algorithms.

By solving these equations or using RL algorithms, an agent can learn the optimal policy to navigate the grid world efficiently.

This simple grid world example illustrates the fundamental components and mathematical foundations of reinforcement learning. In practice, RL problems are often more complex, and various RL algorithms are used to find optimal policies for tasks like game playing, robotics, and recommendation systems.

Reinforcement learning agents learn through interaction with an environment, which means that they make a series of decisions and take actions in response to the environment's feedback to maximize their cumulative reward. Let's explain this concept using a simple example of training an agent to play a game.

Example: Teaching an Agent to Play Chess
Imagine we want to teach an RL agent how to play chess. In this scenario:

1. Agent (RL Learner): The agent is our RL learner, which is a computer program designed to play chess.

2. Environment (Chessboard: The environment, in this case, is a virtual chessboard with pieces arranged as in a standard chess game.

3. State (Game Position): At each time step, the state represents the current position of pieces on the chessboard. The state changes with each move made by the agent or its opponent.

4. Actions (Chess Moves): The actions represent the moves the agent can make in a given state. These are the legal chess moves, such as "pawn to e4" or "knight to f3."

5. Reward (Game Outcome): The reward is the outcome of the game, which can be assigned a numerical value. Winning the game could be rewarded with a positive value (+1), losing with a negative value (-1), and drawing with a neutral value (0).

Now, let's see how the interaction between the agent and the environment occurs:

1. Initialization: The game begins with an initial state, typically the starting position of a chessboard.

2. Agent's Action: The agent selects a chess move based on its current understanding of the game. It might not have any knowledge initially and make random moves.

3. Environment's Response: The environment (chessboard) updates to a new state based on the agent's move. It simulates the opponent's move if the agent is playing against an opponent or uses predefined rules to update the state.

4. Reward Feedback: The environment assigns a reward to the agent based on the outcome of the game. If the agent wins, it receives a positive reward; if it loses, it gets a negative reward; and if the game is a draw, the reward is neutral.

5. Learning and Policy Update: The agent learns from the experience, trying to improve its understanding of the game and make better moves in the future. It adjusts its policy (strategy) based on this feedback.

6. Repeat: Steps 2-5 are repeated for many episodes (games) to accumulate experience and refine the agent's strategy.

Over time, the agent's policy becomes more refined and optimized for playing chess. It learns which moves lead to positive rewards and which ones lead to negative outcomes. It also learns the consequences of its actions, such as understanding how a move in the early game can affect the later stages of the game.

Through this iterative process of interaction with the environment, the reinforcement learning agent becomes increasingly skilled at playing chess and can make more informed decisions. The same concept applies to various other RL applications, from robotics to recommendation systems, where agents learn by interacting with their respective environments and receiving feedback in the form of rewards or penalties.

4.7 State-of-The-Art Reinforcement Learning Models:

Several models have demonstrated exceptional performance in various domains. These models have pushed the boundaries of RL research and are integral to many cutting-edge applications. Here are some notable state-of-the-art RL models:

1. DQN (Deep Q-Network): DQN is one of the pioneering models that combined deep learning with reinforcement learning. It introduced the concept of Q-learning with deep neural networks, making it suitable for solving problems with high-dimensional state spaces.

2. A3C (Asynchronous Advantage Actor-Critic): A3C is an efficient and scalable RL algorithm that combines actor-critic methods with asynchronous training. It's known for its ability to handle both discrete and continuous action spaces.

3. TRPO (Trust Region Policy Optimization): TRPO is an on-policy optimization algorithm that ensures that policy updates do not deviate too far from the previous policy. It is known for its stability and sample efficiency.

4. PPO (Proximal Policy Optimization): PPO is another on-policy optimization algorithm that addresses some of the limitations of TRPO. It is widely used and is known for its ease of implementation and good performance.

5. SAC (Soft Actor-Critic): SAC is an off-policy algorithm for continuous action spaces. It introduces a soft value function and uses an entropy regularization term to encourage exploration.

6. A2C (Advantage Actor-Critic): A2C is a synchronous version of A3C, offering more stability and simplicity. It combines the benefits of actor-critic methods with parallelized training.

7. D4PG (Distributed Distributional Deterministic Policy Gradients): D4PG is an off-policy actor-critic algorithm that introduces distributional value functions. It's designed for handling continuous action spaces and is known for its sample efficiency.

8. Rainbow: Rainbow is an ensemble of reinforcement learning agents that combines multiple techniques like DQN, C51, and prioritized experience replay to achieve superior performance in various tasks.

9. AlphaZero: AlphaZero is an algorithm developed by DeepMind, known for its exceptional performance in board games like chess, shogi, and Go. It uses a combination of deep neural networks and Monte Carlo Tree Search (MCTS) for decision-making.

10. SOTA in Continuous Control: For continuous control tasks, TD3 (Twin Delayed Deep Deterministic Policy Gradients) and SAC (Soft Actor-Critic) have been among the state-of-the-art models, offering superior performance and sample efficiency.

11. CURL (Contrastive Unsupervised Representations for Reinforcement Learning): CURL is a model that combines reinforcement learning with self-supervised learning for improved exploration and representation learning.

Please note that the field of reinforcement learning is highly dynamic, and new models and algorithms may have emerged. Researchers continually work on enhancing RL algorithms to address challenges such as sample efficiency, exploration, and stability. To stay current with the latest developments, I recommend checking the most recent literature and publications in the field of reinforcement learning.

4.8 Implementing in Python

```python
import gym
import numpy as np
import tensorflow as tf
from tensorflow.keras import layers
# Create the CartPole environment
env = gym.make('CartPole-v1')
state_dim = env.observation_space.shape[0]
n_actions = env.action_space.n
```

```python
# Define the Q-Network
model = tf.keras.Sequential([
    layers.Input(shape=(state_dim,)),
    layers.Dense(64, activation='relu'),
    layers.Dense(64, activation='relu'),
    layers.Dense(n_actions, activation='linear')
])
# Compile the model
model.compile(optimizer='adam', loss='mse')
# Hyper parameters
gamma = 0.99  # Discount factor
epsilon = 0.1  # Exploration factor
batch_size = 32
# Training loop
num_episodes = 1000
for episode in range(num_episodes):
    state = env.reset()
    episode_reward = 0

    while True:
        if np.random.rand() < epsilon:
            action = np.random.choice(n_actions)
        else:
            q_values = model.predict(state[None, :])
            action = np.argmax(q_values)
        next_state, reward, done, _ = env.step(action)
        episode_reward += reward
        target = reward + gamma * np.max(model.predict(next_state[None, :]))
        q_values = model.predict(state[None, :])
        q_values[0][action] = target
        model.fit(state[None, :], q_values, verbose=0)
        state = next_state
        if done:
            break
    print(f"Episode: {episode + 1}, Total Reward: {episode_reward}")
# Evaluate the trained model
total_reward = 0
num_eval_episodes = 10
for episode in range(num_eval_episodes):
    state = env.reset()
```

```
while True:
    action = np.argmax(model.predict(state[None, :])
    next_state, reward, done, _ = env.step(action)
    total_reward += reward
    state = next_state
    if done:
        break
average_reward = total_reward / num_eval_episodes
print(f"Average Reward over {num_eval_episodes} evaluation episodes: {average_reward}")
```

This code provides a simple DQN implementation for the CartPole-v1 environment using TensorFlow. Please note that more complex environments and models would require additional components and fine-tuning. Additionally, state-of-the-art models like Rainbow, A3C, and AlphaZero involve more advanced techniques and are typically applied to more challenging tasks. Implementing them would require a more extensive codebase and possibly distributed computing resources.

Exercise Chapter 4:

Multiple Choice

1. What are the four main components of a reinforcement learning agent?

   - ○ A. Policy, value function, state space, and action space

   - ○ B. Policy, value function, reward function, and environment

   - ○ C. Policy, value function, environment, and model

   - ○ D. Policy, value function, reward function, and model

2. What is the goal of a reinforcement learning agent?

   - ○ A. To learn a policy that maximizes the expected reward over time

   - ○ B. To learn a policy that minimizes the expected loss over time

   - ○ C. To learn a policy that maximizes the accuracy of its predictions

   - ○ D. To learn a policy that minimizes the error of its predictions

3. What is the difference between a value function and a policy?

   - ○ A. A value function predicts the expected future reward from a given state, while a policy maps states to actions

   - ○ B. A value function predicts the expected loss from a given state, while a policy maps states to actions

   - ○ C. A value function predicts the expected accuracy of a given action, while a policy maps states to actions

   - ○ D. A value function predicts the expected error of a given action, while a policy maps states to actions

4. What is the difference between an on-policy and an off-policy reinforcement learning algorithm?

   - ○ A. An on-policy algorithm learns from the current policy, while an off-policy algorithm learns from a different policy

   - ○ B. An on-policy algorithm learns from the current state, while an off-policy algorithm learns from a different state

   - ○ C. An on-policy algorithm learns from the current action, while an off-policy algorithm learns from a different action

o   D. An on-policy algorithm learns from the current reward, while an off-policy algorithm learns from a different reward

True/False

1.   Reinforcement learning is a type of supervised learning. (False)

2.   Reinforcement learning agents can learn to perform complex tasks without any prior knowledge of the environment. (True)

3.   Reinforcement learning agents can be used to solve problems in a variety of domains, including robotics, finance, and healthcare. (True)

4.   Reinforcement learning algorithms are always able to find the optimal policy for a given task. (False)

Short Answer

1.   What are some of the different types of reinforcement learning algorithms?

2.   Explain how reinforcement learning can be used to train a robot to walk.

3.   What are some of the challenges of using reinforcement learning in real-world applications?

4.   Describe the process of simulating an environment for reinforcement learning.

Long Answer

1.   Write a blog post about the basics of reinforcement learning.

2.   Implement a simple reinforcement learning algorithm, such as Q-learning, to solve a classic problem, such as the gridworld problem.

3.   Compare the performance of different reinforcement learning algorithms on a specific task.

4.   Write a research paper on the use of reinforcement learning in a specific domain, such as robotics or finance.

Chapter 5: Generative Adversarial Networks (GANs)

5.1 Introduction

Generative Adversarial Networks (GANs) are a class of machine learning models that have gained significant attention for their ability to generate data that closely resembles real-world data. GANs were introduced by Ian Good fellow and his colleagues in 2014 and have since become a powerful tool in various domains, including computer vision, natural language processing, and generative art.

At their core, GANs consist of two neural networks: a generator and a discriminator. The generator's role is to create data, while the discriminator's job is to distinguish between real data and fake data generated by the generator. GANs are trained in a competitive manner, where the generator aims to create data that is indistinguishable from real data, and the discriminator strives to get better at telling real from fake.

Generative Adversarial Networks (GANs) are a type of machine learning model that can be used to generate data that closely resembles real-world data. GANs are trained using a two-player game between two neural networks: a generator and a discriminator.

The generator's goal is to create synthetic data that is indistinguishable from real data. The discriminator's goal is to distinguish between synthetic data and real data.

The generator and discriminator are trained simultaneously. At each iteration, the generator creates a batch of synthetic data, and the discriminator tries to classify each data point as either synthetic or real.

The generator is trained using the feedback from the discriminator. If the discriminator is able to correctly classify a data point as synthetic, then the generator is updated to try to make its synthetic data more realistic.

The discriminator is trained using a supervised learning algorithm. The discriminator is given a set of labeled data, which includes both synthetic and real data. The discriminator is then trained to classify each data point as either synthetic or real.

The training process continues until the generator is able to create synthetic data that is indistinguishable from real data, and the discriminator is unable to distinguish between synthetic data and real data.

GANs have been used to generate a wide variety of data, including images, text, and audio. GANs have also been used to develop new machine learning algorithms for tasks such as image classification and machine translation.

Here are some of the benefits of using GANs:

- GANs can generate data that closely resembles real-world data. This makes GANs useful for a variety of tasks, such as image generation and machine translation.

- GANs can be used to develop new machine learning algorithms. For example, GANs have been used to develop new algorithms for image classification and machine translation.

- GANs are relatively easy to train. Unlike other generative models, GANs do not require a prior distribution over the data that is being generated.

However, there are also some challenges associated with using GANs:

- GANs can be difficult to train. GANs are a type of adversarial network, which means that the generator and discriminator are constantly trying to outsmart each other. This can make it difficult to train GANs to converge on a good solution.

- GANs can be sensitive to the hyper parameters. GANs have a number of hyper parameters that control the training process. It can be difficult to find the right hyper parameters for a particular problem.

- GANs can generate unrealistic data. GANs are trained to generate data that is indistinguishable from real data. However, this does not mean that the data that GANs generate will always be realistic. For example, a GAN trained to generate images of cats may generate images of cats that do not exist in the real world.

Despite these challenges, GANs are a powerful tool for generating data and developing new machine learning algorithms. GANs are used in a variety of domains, including computer vision, machine translation, and natural language processing.

Here are some examples of how GANs are being used in the real world:

- GANs are being used to generate realistic images of people and objects. This technology is being used to develop new video games and movies, and to create new advertising campaigns.

- GANs are being used to improve the quality of machine translation. GANs can be used to generate realistic translations of text, which can be useful for tasks such as translating news articles and business documents.

- GANs are being used to develop new machine learning algorithms for tasks such as image classification and medical diagnosis. GANs can be used to generate synthetic data that can be used to train machine learning algorithms without the need for a large amount of real-world data.

GANs are a rapidly developing field of research, and new applications for GANs are being discovered all the time. GANs have the potential to revolutionize the way that we generate data and develop machine learning algorithms.

5.2 How GANs Work

GANs work by training two neural networks in a two player game: a generator and a discriminator.

The generator's goal is to create synthetic data that is indistinguishable from real data. The discriminator's goal is to distinguish between synthetic data and real data.

The generator and discriminator are trained simultaneously. At each iteration, the generator creates a batch of synthetic data, and the discriminator tries to classify each data point as either synthetic or real.

The generator is trained using the feedback from the discriminator. If the discriminator is able to correctly classify a data point as synthetic, then the generator is updated to try to make its synthetic data more realistic.

The discriminator is trained using a supervised learning algorithm. The discriminator is given a set of labeled data, which includes both synthetic and real data. The discriminator is then trained to classify each data point as either synthetic or real.

The training process continues until the generator is able to create synthetic data that is indistinguishable from real data, and the discriminator is unable to distinguish between synthetic data and real data.

Here is a step-by-step explanation of how GANs work:

1. The generator creates a batch of synthetic data.

2. The discriminator tries to classify each data point in the batch as either synthetic or real.

3. The generator is updated using the feedback from the discriminator.

4. The discriminator is updated using a supervised learning algorithm.

5. Steps 1-4 are repeated until the generator is able to create synthetic data that is indistinguishable from real data, and the discriminator is unable to distinguish between synthetic data and real data.

GANs can be used to generate a wide variety of data, including images, text, and audio. GANs have also been used to develop new machine learning algorithms for tasks such as image classification and machine translation.

Here are some examples of what GANs can generate:

*   Images of people, animals, and objects

*   Text, such as news articles and poems

*   Audio, such as music and speech

GANs are a powerful tool for generating data and developing new machine learning algorithms. GANs are used in a variety of domains, including computer vision, machine translation, and natural language processing.

5.2.1 Generator

The generator network takes random noise as input and generates data samples. It starts with random noise and progressively transforms it into data that resembles the target data distribution. The generator's objective is to create samples that are so convincing that the discriminator can't differentiate them from real data.

5.2.2 Discriminator

The discriminator network's role is to classify whether a given data sample is real (from the true data distribution) or fake (generated by the generator). The discriminator is trained to become better at distinguishing real from fake data.

5.2.3 Adversarial Training

The generator and discriminator are trained in a min-max game. The generator wants to minimize the chance of its data being classified as fake, while the discriminator wants to maximize its accuracy in classifying real and fake data. This adversarial process helps the generator improve over time, generating data that is increasingly convincing.

5.2.4 Training GANs

Training GANs can be challenging and requires careful design. It's essential to find a balance between the generator and discriminator, as an overly powerful generator can render the discriminator useless, and vice versa. Techniques like Wasserstein GANs (WGANs) and progressive training have been introduced to improve GAN training stability.

5.3 Step-by-Step Explanation of GANs

Generative Adversarial Networks (GANs) consist of two neural networks – a generator and a discriminator – engaged in an adversarial training process. The generator's role is to create data that resembles real data, while the discriminator aims to distinguish between real and fake data. Here's how GANs work step by step:

Step 1: Initialization

Both the generator and the discriminator start with random weights. The generator typically takes random noise as input, and the discriminator takes data from the real dataset (real samples) and fake data generated by the generator (fake samples).

Step 2: Generator Generates Data:

The generator takes random noise (a vector) as input and generates fake data samples. Initially, these generated samples are random and don't resemble real data.

Step 3: Discriminator Evaluates Data

The discriminator evaluates both real data samples from the dataset and the fake data generated by the generator. It assigns a probability or score to each sample indicating the likelihood that it's real. In the beginning, the discriminator is not very good at distinguishing real from fake.

Step 4: Training the Discriminator

The discriminator is trained using a binary classification loss function (e.g., cross-entropy). It learns to improve its ability to distinguish between real and fake data samples. It updates its weights to minimize the error in classifying real and fake data.

Step 5: Generator Generates Improved Data

While the discriminator is training, the generator continues to create fake data samples using random noise. As the training progresses, the generator's output improves, making it more challenging for the discriminator to distinguish fake data from real data.

Step 6: Training the Generator

The generator is trained to generate data that can fool the discriminator. It updates its weights to maximize the probability that the discriminator assigns to its fake data as being real. This encourages the generator to produce more realistic data.

Step 7: Adversarial Training

The training process continues with the discriminator and generator engaged in an adversarial game. The generator attempts to create more convincing fake data, while the discriminator works to become better at detecting fake data. This adversarial process repeats for multiple iterations.

Step 8: Convergence

Over time, with each update, the generator and discriminator get better at their respective tasks. Ideally, the generator produces data that is indistinguishable from real data, and the discriminator is unable to differentiate between real and fake samples. This state is called equilibrium or convergence.

Step 9: Generating Data

Once trained, the generator can be used to create new data samples. By providing random noise as input, it generates data that resembles the training data distribution. This generated data can be used for various applications, such as image synthesis, style transfer, and more.

It's important to note that GAN training can be challenging, and it requires careful hyper parameter tuning, architecture selection, and a large dataset. Researchers have introduced variants of GANs, such as Wasserstein GANs (WGANs), to improve training stability.

The effectiveness of GANs in generating high-quality data has made them a valuable tool in areas like computer vision, image synthesis, and creative arts. However, ethical considerations around deepfakes and privacy breaches have also raised important discussions regarding responsible use of this technology.

5.4 Mathematical Model of GAN

The mathematical model of a Generative Adversarial Network (GAN) involves two main components: the generator (G) and the discriminator (D). GANs are trained using an adversarial process where the generator aims to create data that is indistinguishable from real data, while the discriminator aims to distinguish between real and fake data. Let's break down the mathematical model step by step:

1.Generator (G):

- The generator is a neural network represented by a function $G(z)$, where z is a random noise vector drawn from a simple distribution (often Gaussian). $G(z)$ maps the noise vector to a generated data sample.
- The generator's objective is to create data that resembles the real data distribution. It aims to minimize the difference between its generated data and real data, as measured by a loss function.

The generator's objective can be defined as minimizing the following loss:

$$J(G) = -E[\log(D(G(z)))]$$

where:

E represents the expected value over all possible noise vectors z.

$D(G(z))$ is the probability assigned by the discriminator to the generated data.

2. Discriminator (D):

The discriminator is another neural network represented by a function $D(x)$, where x is a data sample. $D(x)$ maps data samples to a probability indicating whether they are real or fake.

The discriminator's objective is to distinguish between real and fake data effectively. It aims to maximize the difference between its classification of real and fake data.

The discriminator's objective can be defined as maximizing the following loss:

$$J(D) = -E[\log(D(x))] - E[\log(1 - D(G(z)))]$$

where:

- E represents the expected value over real data samples (x) and generated data samples (G(z)).

- $D(x)$ is the probability assigned by the discriminator to real data.

- $D(G(z))$ is the probability assigned by the discriminator to generated data.

3. Adversarial Training:

The training process involves an adversarial game between the generator and discriminator. It can be formulated as a minimax optimization problem:

$$\min_G \max_D J(D, G) = -E[\log(D(x))] - E[\log(1 - D(G(z)))]$$

In practice, this minimax optimization problem is typically solved iteratively. The generator and discriminator take turns updating their weights to improve their objectives, leading to a competitive training process. The goal is for the generator to generate data that is indistinguishable from real data, and for the discriminator to be unable to differentiate between real and fake data.

The GAN training process seeks an equilibrium where the generator produces data that is realistic enough to deceive the discriminator. At this equilibrium, the generated data closely matches the real data distribution.

It's important to emphasize that GAN training is highly dependent on architectural choices, hyper parameters, and the specific objective function used. Variants of GANs, such as Wasserstein GANs (WGANs) and progressive GANs, have been introduced to address training challenges and improve stability.

5.5 State-of-the-Art Generative Adversarial Network (GAN) models:

Several GAN models have been developed. These models have made significant advancements in generating high-quality and realistic data in various domains. However, please note that the field of GANs is highly dynamic, and new models may have emerged since then. Here are some notable GAN models up to that point:

StyleGAN 2 (and StyleGAN 3)

Developed by NVIDIA, StyleGAN 2 and its successor StyleGAN 3 are known for their ability to generate highly realistic and customizable faces and images. They introduce progressive growing and style-based techniques.

BigGAN:

BigGAN, developed by Google, is designed for generating high-resolution images. It's known for its impressive image quality and scalability, capable of producing images with exceptional detail.

PGGAN (Progressive GAN):

PGGAN is known for its progressive training approach. It starts with low-resolution images and progressively increases the resolution, resulting in high-quality images.

CycleGAN:

CycleGAN is used for image-to-image translation tasks, allowing style and content transfer between different domains. It has applications in tasks like turning photos into paintings and changing day scenes into night scenes.

StarGAN:

StarGAN is another model for image-to-image translation. It can perform tasks like facial attribute transfer, allowing one model to change multiple attributes in images.

Wasserstein GAN (WGAN):

WGAN introduced a Wasserstein distance-based loss function that significantly improved GAN training stability and encouraged the generation of higher-quality images.

StyleGAN 2-ADA (Adaptive Discriminator Augmentation):

This is an improved version of StyleGAN 2 that introduces data augmentation in the discriminator to improve training stability.

ProGAN (Progressive GAN):

Similar to PGGAN, Progressive GAN uses a progressive training approach for generating high-resolution images with fine details.

BigGAN:

Developed by Google AI, BigGAN focuses on generating high-quality, high-resolution images. It's known for its scalability and the ability to generate high-quality images in various domains.

ALI (Adversarially Learned Inference):

ALI focuses on the generation of high-quality images and introduces a joint training approach for generating data and inferring latent representations.

Self-Attention GAN (SAGAN):

SAGAN incorporates self-attention mechanisms into GAN architectures to capture long-range dependencies in images and improve image quality.

VQ-VAE-2:

While not a traditional GAN, VQ-VAE-2 is a model for discrete latent variable generation and has been used in generating high-quality images and audio.

These GAN models have pushed the boundaries of image generation and manipulation, and they have applications in areas like computer vision, art, and content creation. Keep in mind that GAN research evolves rapidly, and newer models and techniques continue to emerge. For the latest state-of-the-art GAN models, I recommend checking the latest research papers and publications in the field.

4.6 Implementation

4.9.1 StyleGAN2

Implementing StyleGAN2, a highly complex GAN model for generating high-quality images, is an extensive task and would require significant computational resources. It involves working with a pre-trained model and a well-established deep learning framework. To get you started, here's a simplified example using TensorFlow and the official pre-trained StyleGAN2 model:

1. Install Required Libraries:

First, ensure you have the necessary libraries installed, including TensorFlow and the StyleGAN2 repository.

```
pip install tensorflow==1.15  # StyleGAN2 is compatible with TensorFlow 1.x

git clone https://github.com/NVlabs/stylegan2.git

cd stylegan2
```

2. Download Pre-trained Model:

You'll need a pre-trained StyleGAN2 model. You can use a model from the official StyleGAN2 repository, or you can find other pre-trained models available online.

3. Generate Images:

Here's a simple script to generate images using a pre-trained StyleGAN2 model:

```python
import os
import pickle
import numpy as np
import tensorflow as tf
# Set the path to the pre-trained StyleGAN2 model
model_path = 'path/to/pre-trained/stylegan2.pkl'  # Replace with the actual path
# Load the pre-trained StyleGAN2 model
with open(model_path, 'rb') as f: _, _, Gs = pickle.load(f)
# Generate random latent vectors
num_samples = 10
latent_dim = 512
latents = np.random.randn(num_samples, latent_dim)
# Generate images
images = Gs.run(latents, None, truncation_psi=0.7, randomize_noise=False,
output_transform=dict(func=tf.transpose))
# Ensure the output directory exists
output_dir = 'generated_images'
os.makedirs(output_dir, exist_ok=True)
# Save the generated images
for i, image in enumerate(images):
    image = np.clip((image + 1) * 127.5, 0, 255).astype(np.uint8)  # Convert to 8-bit image
    tf.keras.preprocessing.image.save_img(os.path.join(output_dir, f'image_{i}.png'), image[0])
```

In this script, you load a pre-trained StyleGAN2 model, generate random latent vectors, and produce images using the generator (Gs). The generated images are saved in the 'generated_images' directory.

Please note that this is a simplified example for generating images using StyleGAN2. Working with StyleGAN2 for more advanced tasks like style transfer or fine-tuning requires a deeper understanding of GANs and significant computational resources. You may want to explore the official StyleGAN2 repository (https://github.com/NVlabs/stylegan2) and its documentation for more comprehensive usage and customization.

Implementation of BigGAN

Implementing BigGAN from scratch in a single Python script is quite complex due to the model's architecture and the need for significant computational resources. BigGAN is a large-scale GAN model with a complex structure. To work with BigGAN, it's recommended to use pre-trained models and libraries designed for working with large GANs like Hugging Face's Transformers library. Here's an example of how to use a pre-trained BigGAN model from Hugging Face:

1. Install Required Libraries:

Ensure you have the `transformers` library installed.

!pip install transformers

2. Generate Images Using Pre-trained BigGAN:

The following code demonstrates how to use a pre-trained BigGAN model to generate images:

```
from transformers import BigGANTokenizer, BigGANConfig, TFBigGANForGeneration
import tensorflow as tf
import numpy as np
import PIL.Image
import IPython.display as display


# Load a pre-trained BigGAN model and tokenizer
model_name = "biggan-deep-128"  # You can choose other BigGAN variants
tokenizer = BigGANTokenizer.from_pre-trained(model_name)
model = TFBigGANForGeneration.from_pre-trained(model_name)


# Generate random latent vectors
num_samples = 4
latent_dim = model.config.hidden_size
latents = tf.random.normal(shape=(num_samples, latent_dim))


# Generate images from latent vectors
```

```
output = model.generate(latents, return_dict_in_generate=True)

# Post-process and display the generated images
images = output["pixel_values"]
images = (images + 1) / 2.0  # Rescale to [0, 1]

# Display the generated images
for i, image in enumerate(images):
    image = np.array(image * 255, dtype=np.uint8)
    pil_image = PIL.Image.fromarray(image)
    display.display(pil_image)
```

In this code, we use the Hugging Face Transformers library to load a pre-trained BigGAN model. We generate random latent vectors and then use the model to produce images. The generated images are displayed in the IPython notebook.

Please note that the specific model name "biggan-deep-128" can be replaced with other BigGAN variants available in the Hugging Face model hub. Also, generating high-quality images with BigGAN often requires fine-tuning or additional post-processing steps. If you have specific requirements, consider exploring the official BigGAN repository and research papers for more details on working with BigGAN.

Exercise Chapter 5:

Multiple Choice

1. What are the two main components of a GAN?

    o   A. Generator and discriminator

    o   B. Encoder and decoder

    o   C. Policy and value function

    o   D. Environment and agent

2. What is the goal of the generator in a GAN?

    o   A. To generate realistic-looking data

    o   B. To distinguish between real and fake data

    o   C. To learn a policy that maximizes the expected reward

    o   D. To learn a value function that predicts the expected future reward

3. What is the goal of the discriminator in a GAN?

    o   A. To generate realistic-looking data

    o   B. To distinguish between real and fake data

    o   C. To learn a policy that maximizes the expected reward

    o   D. To learn a value function that predicts the expected future reward

4. What are some of the challenges of training GANs?

    o   A. GANs can be unstable and difficult to train

    o   B. GANs can be computationally expensive to train

    o   C. GANs can generate unrealistic-looking data if not trained properly

    o   D. All of the above

True/False

1. GANs can be used to generate any type of data, including images, text, and audio. (True)

2. GANs are always able to generate realistic-looking data. (False)

3. GANs can be used to solve a variety of problems, such as image generation, text translation, and style transfer. (True)

4. GANs are a relatively new technique, and research in this area is still ongoing. (True)

Short Answer

1. What are some of the different types of GAN architectures?

2. Explain how GANs can be used to generate images of human faces.

3. What are some of the ways to improve the stability of GAN training?

4. Describe the process of evaluating the performance of a GAN.

Long Answer

1. Write a blog post about the basics of GANs and their applications.

2. Implement a simple GAN architecture, such as the DCGAN, to generate images of handwritten digits.

3. Compare the performance of different GAN architectures on a specific task, such as image generation or text translation.

4. Write a research paper on the use of GANs in a specific domain, such as art or medicine.

Chapter 6: AutoML.

6.1 Introduction to AutoML

AutoML, short for Automated Machine Learning, is a set of techniques and tools that aims to automate various aspects of the machine learning pipeline. The goal of AutoML is to make machine learning more accessible to individuals and organizations that may not have the expertise or resources to manually design, train, and deploy machine learning models.

AutoML encompasses a wide range of tasks, including data preprocessing, feature engineering, algorithm selection, hyper parameter tuning, model selection, and model evaluation. By automating these processes, AutoML can significantly reduce the barriers to entry for machine learning and democratize the field. This includes tasks such as data preprocessing, feature engineering, model selection, hyper parameter tuning, and model evaluation.

AutoML can help to democratize machine learning by making it accessible to people with limited machine learning expertise. AutoML can also help to improve the efficiency and effectiveness of machine learning projects by automating tasks that are often time-consuming and repetitive.

Here are some of the benefits of using AutoML:

- Increased productivity: AutoML can help to increase the productivity of machine learning teams by automating many of the time-consuming and repetitive tasks involved in machine learning projects.

- Improved model performance: AutoML can help to improve the performance of machine learning models by exploring a wider range of models and hyper parameters than would be possible manually.

- Reduced costs: AutoML can help to reduce the costs of machine learning projects by automating tasks that would otherwise require expensive human experts.

- Increased accessibility: AutoML can make machine learning more accessible to people with limited machine learning expertise.

However, there are also some challenges associated with using AutoML:

- Black box models: AutoML models can be black box models, which means that it can be difficult to understand how the models work and why they make the predictions that they do.

- Data requirements: AutoML models typically require large amounts of data to train effectively.

- Computational requirements: AutoML models can be computationally expensive to train and deploy.

Despite these challenges, AutoML is a promising technology that has the potential to revolutionize the way that machine learning is developed and deployed.

Here are some examples of how AutoML is being used in the real world:

- Google Cloud AutoML: Google Cloud AutoML is a cloud-based AutoML platform that can be used to train and deploy machine learning models for a variety of tasks, including image classification, text classification, and translation.

- Amazon SageMaker Autopilot: Amazon SageMaker Autopilot is a cloud-based AutoML platform that can be used to train and deploy machine learning models for a variety of tasks, including regression, classification, and forecasting.

- H2O Driverless AI: H2O Driverless AI is a commercial AutoML platform that can be used to train and deploy machine learning models for a variety of tasks, including image classification, text classification, and anomaly detection.

AutoML is a rapidly developing field of research, and new AutoML tools and techniques are being developed all the time. AutoML has the potential to make machine learning more accessible, efficient, and effective.

6.2 Technical Background of AutoML

AutoML models are typically trained using a two-stage process:

1. Data exploration and preparation: In the first stage, the AutoML model explores the data and prepares it for training. This may involve tasks such as cleaning the data, handling missing values, and feature engineering.

2. Model selection and hyper parameter tuning: In the second stage, the AutoML model selects a machine learning model and tunes its hyper parameters. The AutoML model may explore a variety of different machine learning models and hyper parameter combinations in order to find the best model for the given dataset.

Once the AutoML model has been trained, it can be used to make predictions on new data.

AutoML models can be implemented using a variety of different techniques. Some common AutoML techniques include:

- Ensemble learning: Ensemble learning is a technique that combines the predictions of multiple machine learning models to produce a more accurate prediction. AutoML models can use ensemble learning to combine the predictions of different machine learning models that have been trained on the same dataset.

- Bayesian optimization: Bayesian optimization is a technique that uses Bayesian statistics to optimize the hyper parameters of a machine learning model. AutoML models can use Bayesian optimization to find the best hyper parameters for a given machine learning model and dataset.

- Neural architecture search: Neural architecture search is a technique that uses machine learning to design new neural network architectures. AutoML models can use neural architecture search to design new machine learning models that are tailored to the specific dataset that they are being trained on.

6.2.1 AutoML Process Model:

Data Preprocessing
AutoML tools often include data cleaning, imputation of missing values, feature scaling, and encoding categorical variables. These processes help ensure that the data is in the right format for model training.

Feature Engineering
Feature engineering is a crucial step in building effective machine learning models. AutoML systems can automate feature selection and transformation, helping identify relevant features and creating new ones.

Algorithm Selection
Different machine learning algorithms are suitable for different types of problems. AutoML tools can automatically select the most appropriate algorithm for a given task, saving users from the need to experiment with various algorithms.

Hyper parameter Tuning
Hyper parameters are settings that control the learning process of a machine learning model. AutoML can automate the search for the best hyper parameters by using techniques like grid search, random search, or Bayesian optimization.

Model Selection
AutoML systems can recommend or automatically select the best-performing model for a given problem. This includes choosing between different types of models, such as decision trees, support vector machines, or neural networks.

Model Evaluation
AutoML evaluates model performance using various metrics and techniques, allowing users to understand how well their models are likely to perform on new, unseen data.

6.4 Use Cases
AutoML has a wide range of use cases across different domains, including:

-Classification and Regression: AutoML is used to automate the creation of predictive models for tasks like image classification, sentiment analysis, and demand forecasting.

-Natural Language Processing: AutoML can automatically build text classification models, machine translation systems, and chatbots.

-Computer Vision: AutoML is used to create object detection, image segmentation, and facial recognition systems.

- Time Series Analysis: AutoML can automate the development of time series forecasting models for financial, medical, and industrial applications.

6.3 Ethical Considerations

As with any automation technology, there are ethical considerations associated with AutoML. These include bias in the data, transparency of model decisions, and the responsible use of machine learning in sensitive applications.

In the following sections, we will delve deeper into the various components of AutoML, explore popular AutoML tools and frameworks, and discuss case studies and best practices for successful AutoML implementations.

6.4 How AutoML Works

AutoML is a complex field that involves various techniques and processes. Below, we'll explore some of the fundamental mechanisms behind AutoML.

6.4.1 Automated Model Selection

AutoML platforms use automated methods to select the best machine learning model for a specific problem. These methods often involve training and evaluating multiple models to determine which one performs best on the given dataset. Commonly used algorithms include decision trees, random forests, support vector machines, and neural networks.

6.4.2 Hyper Parameter Optimization

Hyper parameters are crucial settings for machine learning algorithms. AutoML tools can automatically search for the optimal combination of hyper parameters, ensuring that models perform at their best. Techniques like grid search, random search, and Bayesian optimization are used to find the right set of hyper parameters.

6.4.3 Feature Engineering

Feature engineering involves creating and selecting relevant input features for machine learning models. AutoML platforms can automate this process by selecting features based on their importance, transforming features, and creating new ones. This simplifies the feature engineering stage and enhances model performance.

6.4.4 Automated Data Preprocessing

Data preprocessing includes tasks such as data cleaning, scaling, encoding categorical variables, and handling missing values. AutoML systems can automate these tasks, ensuring that the input data is in the right format for machine learning.

6.4.5 Model Evaluation and Validation

AutoML tools assess model performance using various metrics and techniques. They perform cross-validation, split data into training and testing sets, and use techniques like k-fold cross-validation to ensure that models generalize well to unseen data.

6.5 AutoML Frameworks and Tools

Several AutoML frameworks and tools are available to help users with automated machine learning tasks. Some of the popular ones include:

1. Auto-sklearn: An automated machine learning toolkit that uses Bayesian optimization and meta-learning.

2. H2O.ai: A platform offering AutoML capabilities, including automatic data preprocessing and hyper parameter tuning.

3. Google AutoML: A suite of tools for various machine learning tasks, including AutoML Vision, AutoML Natural Language, and AutoML Tables.

4. TPOT (Tree-based Pipeline Optimization Tool): A Python library that uses genetic programming to optimize machine learning pipelines.

5. Auto-Keras: An open-source library for automated machine learning using neural architecture search.

6. DataRobot: A comprehensive platform for automated machine learning, feature engineering, and model deployment.

6.8 Use Cases of AutoML

AutoML has a wide range of practical applications, including:

1. Financial Services: Predictive modeling for credit scoring, fraud detection, and investment strategies.

2. Healthcare: Automated diagnosis, patient outcome prediction, and drug discovery.

3. Retail: Demand forecasting, recommendation systems, and inventory management.

4. Manufacturing: Quality control, predictive maintenance, and supply chain optimization.

5. Natural Language Processing (NLP): Text classification, sentiment analysis, and chatbots.

6. Computer Vision: Object detection, image segmentation, and facial recognition.

6.9 Challenges and Ethical Considerations

AutoML is not without its challenges and ethical considerations. Some key challenges include:

- Black-Box Models: Automated machine learning systems can produce complex models that are difficult to interpret, raising concerns about transparency.

- Data Quality: The effectiveness of AutoML heavily relies on the quality of the input data. Biased or noisy data can result in biased models.

- Lack of Control: AutoML tools may limit the control that experts have over the model development process.

Ethical considerations include addressing bias in training data, ensuring model fairness, and being transparent about the automated nature of the machine learning process.

In the following sections, we will explore specific use cases of AutoML, showcase real-world applications, and discuss best practices for adopting and implementing AutoML effectively.

6.10 Mathematical Model

AutoML, or Automated Machine Learning, is not represented by a single mathematical model but rather encompasses a collection of techniques and processes to automate various components of the machine learning pipeline. Below, we'll discuss some of the mathematical concepts and algorithms involved in AutoML processes:

1. Algorithm Selection:

  - Mathematical models used: Cross-validation, statistical tests.

  - In AutoML, algorithms are often evaluated based on performance metrics like accuracy, F1 score, or mean squared error. Cross-validation is used to assess how well algorithms generalize to unseen data. Statistical tests, such as t-tests or paired comparisons, can be used to determine if one algorithm significantly outperforms another.

2. Hyper parameter Optimization:

  - Mathematical models used: Optimization algorithms, search spaces.

  - Hyper parameter optimization involves searching for the best combination of hyper parameters for a given machine learning algorithm. Optimization algorithms like Bayesian optimization or genetic algorithms are employed to explore the hyper parameter search space efficiently.

3. Feature Engineering:

  - Mathematical models used: Feature selection, dimensionality reduction, correlation analysis.

  - Feature engineering includes techniques like mutual information, principal component analysis (PCA), or correlation analysis to identify and select relevant features. These techniques often involve mathematical concepts related to linear algebra and statistics.

4. Data Preprocessing:

  - Mathematical models used: Statistical imputation, scaling, normalization.

- Data preprocessing involves techniques like imputing missing values, scaling features, and encoding categorical variables. Statistical methods for imputation may include mean imputation, median imputation, or regression-based imputation.

5. Model Evaluation:

   - Mathematical models used: Loss functions, cross-validation, statistical tests.

   - Model evaluation includes the calculation of loss functions (e.g., mean squared error or cross-entropy) to assess model performance. Cross-validation is used to estimate how well a model generalizes to unseen data, and statistical tests can determine if differences in performance are significant.

6. Bayesian Optimization:

   - Mathematical models used: Gaussian processes, acquisition functions.

   - Bayesian optimization is a common approach in AutoML for hyper parameter tuning. It uses Gaussian processes to model the objective function (model performance) and acquisition functions (e.g., expected improvement) to select the next set of hyper parameters to evaluate.

7. Genetic Algorithms:

   - Mathematical models used: Population-based optimization, selection, crossover, mutation.

   - Genetic algorithms are used for hyper parameter optimization and feature selection in AutoML. They apply principles of natural selection, including selection, crossover (recombination), and mutation, to evolve   solutions   that   improve   model   performance.
8. Ensemble Methods:

   - Mathematical models used: Weighted averaging, voting.

   - Ensemble methods, such as bagging and boosting, combine multiple machine learning models to create a more robust and accurate model. They often use mathematical concepts like weighted averaging or voting to combine predictions.

AutoML is a field that leverages various mathematical and statistical techniques to automate the machine learning pipeline. While there isn't a single overarching mathematical model for AutoML, the field draws from a wide range of mathematical concepts to streamline and optimize the machine learning process.

6.11 State-of—the-Art AutoML frameworks and models:

that were considered state-of-the-art in the field of automated machine learning. These frameworks aim to automate various aspects of the machine learning pipeline, including data preprocessing, feature engineering, algorithm selection, hyper parameter tuning, and model selection. Here are some of the prominent AutoML models and frameworks, along with brief explanations:

1. AutoML-GAN:

AutoML-GAN is an AutoML framework that leverages the power of Generative Adversarial Networks (GANs) to automate the creation of machine learning models. It focuses on automating the design and selection of neural network architectures.

2. Auto-sklearn:

Auto-sklearn is an automated machine learning toolkit built on top of scikit-learn. It employs Bayesian optimization and meta-learning to choose the best machine learning pipeline for a given dataset, including data preprocessing and algorithm selection.

3. H2O.ai:

H2O.ai offers an AutoML platform that provides automatic feature engineering, hyper parameter tuning, and model selection. It includes AutoML capabilities for various tasks and is known for its ease of use and scalability.

4. Google Cloud AutoML:

Google Cloud AutoML provides a suite of tools for different machine learning tasks, including AutoML Vision, AutoML Natural Language, and AutoML Tables. It allows users to build custom machine learning models without extensive expertise.

5. TPOT (Tree-based Pipeline Optimization Tool):

TPOT is a Python library that uses genetic programming to automate the selection of machine learning pipelines. It searches for the best combination of data preprocessing steps, feature engineering, and algorithms.

6. Auto-Keras:

Explanation: Auto-Keras is an open-source library that uses neural architecture search (NAS) to automatically design deep learning models. It's particularly well-suited for tasks like image classification and natural language processing.

7. DataRobot:

DataRobot is a comprehensive automated machine learning platform that offers end-to-end automation, from data preprocessing to model deployment. It provides a user-friendly interface and aims to democratize machine learning.

8. Microsoft Azure AutoML:

Azure AutoML is part of the Microsoft Azure cloud ecosystem and offers automated machine learning capabilities for a variety of tasks, including classification, regression, and time series forecasting.

9. D3M (Data Driven Discovery of Models):

D3M is a program that aims to automate machine learning by providing a range of tools and techniques to automatically select and optimize models. It focuses on democratizing machine learning research.

10. AutoAI (IBM Watson AutoAI):

AutoAI, part of IBM Watson, offers automated model selection, hyper parameter tuning, and feature engineering. It's designed to make machine learning accessible to business users and data scientists alike.

These AutoML models and frameworks differ in their approaches and capabilities. They are designed to simplify the machine learning process, making it more accessible to a broader audience and improving the efficiency and effectiveness of machine learning applications. Keep in mind that the field of AutoML is rapidly evolving, and new models and frameworks may have emerged since my last update.

Exercise Chapter 6:

Multiple Choice

1. What is AutoML?

   - A. A machine learning technique that automates the process of building and deploying machine learning models.

   - B. A cloud-based platform that provides a variety of machine learning tools and services.

   - C. A software library that makes it easy to train and deploy machine learning models.

   - D. All of the above.

2. What are some of the benefits of using AutoML?

   - A. AutoML can reduce the time and effort required to build and deploy machine learning models.

   - B. AutoML can make machine learning accessible to people with less expertise in machine learning.

   - C. AutoML can improve the performance of machine learning models by automating the hyperparameter optimization process.

- D. All of the above.

3. What are some of the challenges of using AutoML?

- A. AutoML models may not be as performant as models trained by hand by experienced machine learning engineers.

- B. AutoML models may be more difficult to interpret and explain than models trained by hand.

- C. AutoML models may be more susceptible to bias than models trained by hand.

- D. All of the above.

True/False

1. AutoML can be used to build models for a variety of machine learning tasks, including classification, regression, and clustering. (True)

2. AutoML is a completely hands-off process. There is no need for any human intervention in the model building and deployment process. (False)

3. AutoML is a relatively new technology, and research in this area is still ongoing. (True)

4. AutoML is only available on cloud platforms. (False)

Short Answer

1. What are some of the different types of AutoML tools and platforms?

2. Explain how AutoML can be used to build a model to predict customer churn.

3. What are some of the ways to improve the performance and interpretability of AutoML models?

4. Describe the process of evaluating the performance of an AutoML model.

Long Answer

1. Write a blog post about the basics of AutoML and its applications.

2. Implement a simple AutoML model to solve a classic machine learning problem, such as the MNIST handwritten digit classification problem.

3. Compare the performance of different AutoML tools and platforms on a specific task, such as image classification or text translation.

4. Write a research paper on the use of AutoML in a specific domain, such as healthcare or finance.

Chapter 7: Ensemble Learning

7.1 Introduction to Ensemble Learning

Ensemble learning is a powerful machine learning technique that combines the predictions of multiple models to produce a more accurate and robust result than any individual model. The idea behind ensemble learning is to leverage the collective intelligence of multiple models to improve overall predictive performance.

Ensemble methods have gained popularity in various machine learning competitions and real-world applications because they often lead to better generalization and higher accuracy. In this chapter, we will explore the fundamentals of ensemble learning, different ensemble techniques, and their applications.

Why Ensemble Learning?

The core concept of ensemble learning is based on the wisdom of the crowd. It is a well-known principle in machine learning that different models might make different errors. By combining their predictions, ensemble models can reduce individual errors and produce more reliable outcomes. Key benefits of ensemble learning include:

1. Improved Accuracy: Ensemble models often outperform single models by aggregating their predictions.

2. Increased Robustness: Ensembles are less prone to over-fitting and can adapt to diverse data patterns.

3. Mitigation of Bias: Ensemble models can help reduce bias in predictions by averaging out errors from individual models.

4. Enhanced Stability: Ensembles are more stable and less sensitive to minor variations in the training data.

7.2 Types of Ensemble Learning

Ensemble learning is a machine learning technique that combines the predictions of multiple machine learning models to produce a more accurate prediction. Ensemble learning models are typically more accurate than individual machine learning models because they are able to learn from the strengths and weaknesses of each individual model.

There are two main types of ensemble learning: bagging and boosting.

- Bagging: Bagging is a type of ensemble learning that works by training multiple machine learning models on different subsets of the training data. The predictions of the individual models are then averaged to produce the final prediction. Bagging is effective at reducing the variance of the predictions, which can lead to improved accuracy.

- Boosting: Boosting is a type of ensemble learning that works by training multiple machine learning models sequentially. Each model is trained on the errors of the previous model. Boosting is effective at reducing the bias of the predictions, which can also lead to improved accuracy.

Within these two main categories, there are a number of different ensemble learning algorithms. Some of the most popular ensemble learning algorithms include:

- Random forest: Random forest is a bagging algorithm that trains multiple decision trees on different subsets of the training data. Random forests are very effective at reducing variance and improving accuracy.

- Gradient boosting: Gradient boosting is a boosting algorithm that trains multiple decision trees sequentially. Gradient boosting is very effective at reducing bias and improving accuracy.

- AdaBoost: AdaBoost is a boosting algorithm that trains multiple decision stumps sequentially. AdaBoost is a relatively simple algorithm, but it can be very effective at improving the accuracy of machine learning models.

Ensemble learning algorithms can be used for a variety of machine learning tasks, including classification, regression, and anomaly detection. Ensemble learning algorithms are widely used in practice because they are able to produce accurate predictions for a wide range of problems.

Here are some examples of how ensemble learning algorithms are used in the real world:

- Recommendation systems: Ensemble learning algorithms are used in recommendation systems to recommend products, movies, and other items to users.

- Fraud detection: Ensemble learning algorithms are used in fraud detection systems to identify fraudulent transactions.

- Medical diagnosis: Ensemble learning algorithms are used in medical diagnosis systems to help doctors diagnose diseases.

Ensemble learning is a powerful technique that can be used to improve the accuracy of machine learning models. Ensemble learning algorithms are widely used in practice because they are able to produce accurate predictions for a wide range of problems.

7.3 Ensemble Learning Process
Several ensemble techniques are used to combine the predictions of base models, including:

1. Voting: In this technique, each base model makes a prediction, and the final prediction is determined by majority voting.

2. Averaging: The predictions of base models are averaged to produce the final prediction. This is commonly used in regression tasks.

3. Weighted Averaging: Similar to averaging, but each base model's prediction is weighted differently based on its performance.

4. Stacking: Stacking involves training a meta-model (often a simple linear regression model) that takes the predictions of base models as input and learns to make the final prediction.

7.4 Applications of Ensemble Learning

Ensemble learning finds applications in various domains:

1. Classification: Ensemble models are used for tasks like image classification, spam detection, and sentiment analysis.

2. Regression: In regression tasks, ensemble models can predict continuous values, such as house prices and stock prices.

3. Anomaly Detection: Ensemble methods are employed to detect anomalies in data, which is essential for fraud detection and network security.

4. Ranking and Recommendation: Ensemble techniques are used to rank products and provide personalized recommendations in e-commerce and streaming platforms.

5. Natural Language Processing: In NLP, ensemble models improve tasks like text classification, machine translation, and sentiment analysis.

7.5 Bagging (Bootstrap Aggregating):

Bagging is a technique that aims to reduce variance. It involves training multiple base models independently on different random subsets of the training data and then averaging their predictions. The most well-known algorithm for bagging is Random Forest. Bagging, also known as bootstrap aggregating, is a machine learning technique that combines the predictions of multiple machine learning models to produce a more accurate prediction. Bagging works by training multiple machine learning models on different subsets of the training data. The predictions of the individual models are then averaged to produce the final prediction.

Bagging is effective at reducing the variance of the predictions, which can lead to improved accuracy. Variance is a measure of how much the predictions of a machine learning model vary. A machine learning model with high variance is more likely to over fit the training data and perform poorly on new data. Bagging reduces the variance of the predictions by averaging the predictions of multiple machine learning models that have been trained on different subsets of the training data.

Bagging is a simple and effective ensemble learning technique. It is easy to implement and can be used with a variety of different machine learning algorithms. Bagging is widely used in practice because it is able to produce accurate predictions for a wide range of problems.

Here is a step-by-step explanation of how bagging works:

1. Sample the training data with replacement to create multiple subsets of the training data.

2. Train a machine learning model on each subset of the training data.

3. Make predictions on new data using each of the trained machine learning models.

4. Average the predictions of the individual machine learning models to produce the final prediction.

Bagging can be used for a variety of machine learning tasks, including classification, regression, and anomaly detection. Bagging is particularly effective for classification tasks.

Here are some of the benefits of using bagging:

- Reduced variance: Bagging reduces the variance of the predictions, which can lead to improved accuracy.

- Easy to implement: Bagging is a simple and easy-to-implement ensemble learning technique.

- Versatile: Bagging can be used with a variety of different machine learning algorithms.

However, there are also some challenges associated with using bagging:

- Computational requirements: Bagging can be computationally expensive, especially for large datasets.

- Over-fitting: Bagging can lead to Over-fitting if the training data is small.

Despite these challenges, bagging is a powerful ensemble learning technique that can be used to improve the accuracy of machine learning models. Bagging is widely used in practice because it is able to produce accurate predictions for a wide range of problems.

Here are some examples of how bagging is used in the real world:

- Recommendation systems: Bagging is used in recommendation systems to recommend products, movies, and other items to users.

- Fraud detection: Bagging is used in fraud detection systems to identify fraudulent transactions.

- Medical diagnosis: Bagging is used in medical diagnosis systems to help doctors diagnose diseases.

Example:

Let's take the following sample data in a table:

Feature 1	Feature 2	Label
1	2	0

3	4	1
5	6	0
7	8	1
9	10	0

To apply the bagging algorithm to this data, we will follow these steps:

1. Sample the training data with replacement to create multiple subsets of the training data.

For example, we can create the following subsets of the training data:

Subset 1: {1, 2, 3, 5, 7, 9}

Subset 2: {1, 3, 4, 6, 8, 10}

Subset 3: {2, 3, 4, 5, 7, 8}

2. Train a machine learning model on each subset of the training data.

For example, we can train a decision tree model on each subset of the training data.

3. Make predictions on new data using each of the trained machine learning models.

For example, let's say we have a new data point with the following features:

Feature 1 = 11

Feature 2 = 12

We can use each of the trained decision tree models to make a prediction on this new data point.

4. Average the predictions of the individual machine learning models to produce the final prediction.

For example, the predictions of the three decision tree models on the new data point are:

Decision tree 1: 0

Decision tree 2: 1

Decision tree 3: 0

The average of these predictions is 0.5, so the final prediction is 0.5.

This means that the model is 50% sure that the new data point belongs to class 0 and 50% sure that it belongs to class 1.

Bagging can be used with a variety of different machine learning algorithms. In this example, we used decision trees, but we could also have used other algorithms, such as logistic regression or support vector machines.

Bagging is a powerful ensemble learning technique that can be used to improve the accuracy of machine learning models. Bagging is widely used in practice because it is able to produce accurate predictions for a wide range of problems.

7.6 Boosting:

Boosting is a machine learning technique that combines the predictions of multiple machine learning models to produce a more accurate prediction. Boosting works by training multiple machine learning models sequentially, with each model trying to correct the errors of the previous model.

Boosting is a technique that focuses on reducing bias. It involves training multiple base models sequentially, where each subsequent model corrects the errors of the previous ones. AdaBoost, Gradient Boosting, and XGBoost are popular boosting algorithms.

Boosting is effective at reducing the bias of the predictions, which can lead to improved accuracy. Bias is a measure of how far the predictions of a machine learning model are from the true values. A machine learning model with high bias is more likely to underfit the training data and perform poorly on new data. Boosting reduces the bias of the predictions by training multiple machine learning models sequentially, with each model trying to correct the errors of the previous model.

Boosting is a more complex ensemble learning technique than bagging, but it can also produce more accurate predictions. Boosting is often used for classification tasks, but it can also be used for regression tasks.

Here is a step-by-step explanation of how boosting works:

1. Train a weak learner on the training data. A weak learner is a machine learning model that is only slightly better than random chance.

2. Weight the training data based on the predictions of the weak learner. Data points that the weak learner misclassified are given higher weights.

3. Train another weak learner on the weighted training data.

4. Repeat steps 2 and 3 until the desired accuracy is achieved.

5. Combine the predictions of the weak learners to produce the final prediction.

The most common boosting algorithm is AdaBoost. AdaBoost works by training a sequence of decision stumps. A decision stump is a simple decision tree with only one node. AdaBoost is very effective at reducing bias and improving accuracy.

Here are some of the benefits of using boosting:

- Reduced bias: Boosting reduces the bias of the predictions, which can lead to improved accuracy.

- Versatile: Boosting can be used for a variety of machine learning tasks, including classification and regression.

- Powerful: Boosting can produce very accurate predictions, even for complex problems.

However, there are also some challenges associated with using boosting:

- Computational requirements: Boosting can be computationally expensive, especially for large datasets.

- Over-fitting: Boosting can lead to Over-fitting if the training data is small.

Despite these challenges, boosting is a powerful ensemble learning technique that has been used to achieve state-of-the-art results on many machine learning problems.

Here are some examples of how boosting is used in the real world:

- Recommendation systems: Boosting is used in recommendation systems to recommend products, movies, and other items to users.

- Fraud detection: Boosting is used in fraud detection systems to identify fraudulent transactions.

- Medical diagnosis: Boosting is used in medical diagnosis systems to help doctors diagnose diseases.

Boosting is a powerful ensemble learning technique that can be used to improve the accuracy of machine learning models. Boosting is widely used in practice because it is able to produce accurate predictions for a wide range of problems.

Let's take the following sample data in a table:

Feature 1	Feature 2	Label
1	2	0
3	4	1
5	6	0
7	8	1
9	10	0

To apply the boosting algorithm to this data, we will follow these steps:

1. Initialize the weights of all data points to be equal.

2. Train a weak learner on the training data, weighted by the weights of the data points.

3. Update the weights of the data points based on the predictions of the weak learner. Data points that the weak learner misclassified are given higher weights.

4. Repeat steps 2 and 3 until the desired accuracy is achieved.

5. Combine the predictions of the weak learners to produce the final prediction.

For example, let's say we want to use the AdaBoost boosting algorithm to train a classifier on this data. AdaBoost works by training a sequence of decision stumps. A decision stump is a simple decision tree with only one node.

Here is a step-by-step explanation of how to train an AdaBoost classifier on the sample data:

1. Initialize the weights of all data points to be equal.

2. Train a decision stump on the training data, weighted by the weights of the data points.

3. Update the weights of the data points based on the predictions of the decision stump. Data points that the decision stump misclassified are given higher weights.

4. Repeat steps 2 and 3 until the desired accuracy is achieved.

5. Combine the predictions of the decision stumps to produce the final prediction.

For example, let's say we train 10 decision stumps. The following table shows the predictions of the 10 decision stumps on the training data:

Data point	Decision stump 1	Decision stump 2	Decision stump 3	...	Decision stump 10
1	0	0	0	...	0
2	0	1	0	...	0
3	1	1	1	...	1
4	1	1	1	...	1
5	0	0	0	...	0

To combine the predictions of the decision stumps, we can use the following weighted majority vote:

Final prediction = argmax_class(sum_{i=1}^N w_i * stump_i(x))

where:

- argmax_class(x) returns the class with the highest predicted probability

- N is the number of decision stumps

- w_i is the weight of decision stump i

- stump_i(x) is the prediction of decision stump i on data point x

Using this weighted majority vote, the final prediction for each data point is as follows:

Data point	Final prediction
1	0
2	0
3	1
4	1
5	0

As you can see, the AdaBoost classifier is able to correctly classify all of the data points in the training set.

Boosting is a powerful ensemble learning technique that can be used to train very accurate classifiers, even for complex problems. Boosting is widely used in practice in a variety of domains, including computer vision, natural language processing, and fraud detection.

Exercise Chapter 7

Multiple Choice

1. What is ensemble learning?

   o A. A machine learning technique that combines multiple models to produce a more accurate prediction.

   o B. A cloud-based platform that provides a variety of machine learning tools and services.

   o C. A software library that makes it easy to train and deploy machine learning models.

   o D. All of the above.

2. What are some of the benefits of using ensemble learning?

   o A. Ensemble learning can improve the accuracy of machine learning models.

   o B. Ensemble learning can reduce the overfitting of machine learning models.

   o C. Ensemble learning can make machine learning models more robust to noise and outliers.

   o D. All of the above.

3. What are some of the challenges of using ensemble learning?

   o A. Ensemble learning models can be more computationally expensive to train and deploy than individual models.

   o B. Ensemble learning models can be more difficult to interpret and explain than individual models.

   o C. Ensemble learning is not always effective for all machine learning tasks.

   o D. All of the above.

True/False

1. There are two main types of ensemble learning methods: bagging and boosting. (True)

2. Bagging works by creating multiple training datasets from the original training dataset by sampling with replacement. (True)

3. Boosting works by creating a sequence of models, where each model is trained on the residuals of the previous model. (True)

4. Ensemble learning methods can be used with any type of machine learning model, including linear regression, decision trees, and support vector machines. (True)

Short Answer

1. What are some of the different types of ensemble learning methods?

2. Explain how bagging can be used to improve the performance of a decision tree model.

3. What are some of the ways to improve the interpretability of ensemble learning models?

4. Describe the process of evaluating the performance of an ensemble learning model.

Long Answer

1. Write a blog post about the basics of ensemble learning and its applications.

2. Implement a simple ensemble learning model, such as bagging or boosting, to solve a classic machine learning problem, such as the MNIST handwritten digit classification problem.

3. Compare the performance of different ensemble learning methods on a specific task, such as image classification or text translation.

4. Write a research paper on the use of ensemble learning in a specific domain, such as healthcare or finance.

Chapter 8: Self-Supervised Learning

8.1 Introduction to Self-Supervised Learning

Self-supervised learning (SSL) is a type of machine learning where the model learns to perform a task without the need for human-labeled data. SSL algorithms learn by exploiting the inherent structure and relationships in the unlabeled data. In traditional supervised learning, models require labeled data to learn meaningful representations and make predictions. However, acquiring labeled data is often costly and time-consuming. Self-Supervised Learning addresses this limitation by enabling models to learn from the data itself without external annotations.

There are two main types of SSL algorithms:

- Contrastive learning: Contrastive learning algorithms learn by contrasting positive and negative examples of the data. For example, a contrastive learning algorithm for image classification might learn to distinguish between images of a cat and images of a dog.

- Predictive learning: Predictive learning algorithms learn by predicting some aspect of the data. For example, a predictive learning algorithm for image classification might learn to predict the next pixel in an image sequence.

SSL algorithms are often used to pre-train machine learning models before they are fine-tuned on a supervised learning task. This can help to improve the performance of the model on the supervised learning task, even if the amount of labeled data is limited.

Here are some of the benefits of using SSL:

- Reduced need for labeled data: SSL algorithms do not require labeled data to train, which can significantly reduce the cost and time required to develop machine learning models.

- Improved performance on supervised learning tasks: SSL algorithms can be used to pre-train machine learning models before they are fine-tuned on a supervised learning task. This can help to improve the performance of the model on the supervised learning task, even if the amount of labeled data is limited.

- Ability to learn from large amounts of unlabeled data: SSL algorithms can be used to learn from large amounts of unlabeled data, which is often available in abundance. This can help to improve the performance and generalization ability of machine learning models.

However, there are also some challenges associated with using SSL:

- Difficult to design SSL algorithms: Designing SSL algorithms that can learn effectively from unlabeled data is a challenging task.

- Can be computationally expensive: Training SSL algorithms can be computationally expensive, especially for large datasets.

- Can lead to over-fitting: SSL algorithms can lead to over-fitting if they are not trained carefully.

Despite these challenges, SSL is a promising machine learning technique that has the potential to revolutionize the way that machine learning models are developed. SSL algorithms are already being used to achieve state-of-the-art results on a variety of machine learning tasks, including image classification, natural language processing, and computer vision.

Here are some examples of how SSL is being used in the real world:

- Self-driving cars: SSL is used to train self-driving cars to learn from the vast amount of unlabeled sensor data that they collect.

- Medical diagnosis: SSL is used to train medical diagnosis systems to learn from unlabeled medical images and data.

- Recommendation systems: SSL is used to train recommendation systems to learn from unlabeled user data.

Overall, SSL is a powerful and versatile machine learning technique that has the potential to be used in a wide range of applications.

In this chapter, we will explore the concept, principles, and techniques of Self-Supervised Learning, as well as its applications across various domains.

8.2 Principles of Self-Supervised Learning

The fundamental idea behind Self-Supervised Learning is to design auxiliary tasks that leverage the inherent structure and context within the data. These auxiliary tasks serve as a source of self-generated supervision signals. Key principles of Self-Supervised Learning include:

1. Representation Learning: Self-Supervised Learning focuses on learning representations or features that capture the underlying structure in the data. These learned representations can be used for downstream tasks.

2. Auxiliary Tasks: Self-Supervised Learning relies on auxiliary tasks, also known as pretext tasks, that require the model to predict or generate parts of the data. Examples include image inpainting, word prediction in text, and audio reconstruction.

3. Contrastive Learning: Contrastive learning is a popular approach within Self-Supervised Learning. It involves training the model to differentiate between positive samples (e.g., different parts of the same image) and negative samples (e.g., random images or text). By maximizing the similarity between positives and minimizing it between negatives, the model learns meaningful representations.

4. Data Augmentation: Data augmentation is often used to create different views of the same data. By applying transformations or perturbations to the data, models learn to be invariant to such changes and focus on the underlying content.

5. Transfer Learning: Self-Supervised Learning is closely related to transfer learning. The representations learned in self-supervised tasks can be transferred to downstream tasks with smaller amounts of labeled data, improving their performance.

8.4 The Foundation of Self-Supervised Learning

The mathematical foundations of Self-Supervised Learning are based on the design of pretext tasks and the principles of contrastive learning. Let's explore these foundations:

84.1 Pretext Tasks

Pretext tasks are auxiliary tasks used in Self-Supervised Learning to generate supervision signals from unlabeled data. These tasks are designed to encourage the model to learn meaningful representations. Some common pretext tasks include:

1. Image In-painting: Given an image with a missing region, the model is trained to predict the missing part. This encourages the model to understand the context within the image.

2. Text Auto-encoding: In Natural Language Processing, models predict missing words or phrases in sentences. For example, a model might predict the middle word in a sentence given the surrounding words.

3. Temporal Order Prediction: In sequential data, models predict the correct order of elements, such as frames in a video. This task encourages the model to capture temporal dependencies.

4. Contrastive Learning: Contrastive learning is a central concept in Self-Supervised Learning. The model is trained to pull together similar samples and push apart dissimilar samples in a feature space. This is typically achieved through a loss function that maximizes the similarity between positive samples (e.g., different views of the same data) and minimizes the similarity between negative samples (e.g., random data).

8.4.2 Contrastive Learning

Contrastive Learning is a fundamental principle in Self-Supervised Learning. The key idea is to embed data points into a feature space and encourage the model to learn representations that are close for similar data and distant for dissimilar data.

Contrastive learning is a type of self-supervised learning that learns by contrasting positive and negative examples of the data. For example, a contrastive learning algorithm for image classification might learn to distinguish between images of a cat and images of a dog.

Contrastive learning algorithms typically work by training a model to predict whether two data points are similar or not. The model is trained on a set of positive and negative pairs. Positive pairs are data points that are similar, such as two images of the same cat. Negative pairs are data points that are not similar, such as an image of a cat and an image of a dog.

The model is trained to maximize the probability of predicting that positive pairs are similar and minimize the probability of predicting that negative pairs are similar. This can be done using a variety of different loss functions, such as the contrastive loss function.

Once the model is trained, it can be used to generate representations of data points that are useful for a variety of machine learning tasks. For example, the representations learned by a contrastive learning algorithm for image classification can be used to train a classifier to distinguish between different types of images.

Contrastive learning is a powerful technique that can be used to learn from large amounts of unlabeled data. It has been shown to achieve state-of-the-art results on a variety of machine learning tasks, including image classification, natural language processing, and computer vision.

Here are some of the advantages of using contrastive learning:

- It can be used to learn from large amounts of unlabeled data: Contrastive learning algorithms do not require labeled data to train, which can significantly reduce the cost and time required to develop machine learning models.

- It can be used to learn useful representations of data: Contrastive learning algorithms learn representations of data points that are useful for a variety of machine learning tasks.

- It is a versatile technique: Contrastive learning algorithms can be used with a variety of different machine learning algorithms.

However, there are also some challenges associated with using contrastive learning:

- Designing contrastive learning algorithms can be challenging: Designing contrastive learning algorithms that can learn effectively from unlabeled data is a challenging task.

- Training contrastive learning algorithms can be computationally expensive: Training contrastive learning algorithms can be computationally expensive, especially for large datasets.

- Contrastive learning algorithms can lead to over-fitting: Contrastive learning algorithms can lead to over-fitting if they are not trained carefully.

Despite these challenges, contrastive learning is a promising machine learning technique that has the potential to revolutionize the way that machine learning models are developed. Contrastive learning algorithms are already being used to achieve state-of-the-art results on a variety of machine learning tasks, including image classification, natural language processing, and computer vision.

Here are some examples of how contrastive learning is being used in the real world:

- Self-driving cars: Contrastive learning is used to train self-driving cars to learn from the vast amount of unlabeled sensor data that they collect.

- Medical diagnosis: Contrastive learning is used to train medical diagnosis systems to learn from unlabeled medical images and data.

- Recommendation systems: Contrastive learning is used to train recommendation systems to learn from unlabeled user data.

Overall, contrastive learning is a powerful and versatile machine learning technique that has the potential to be used in a wide range of applications.

8.5 Implementing Self-Supervised Learning

Implementing Self-Supervised Learning involves creating pretext tasks, designing a contrastive loss function, and training models on unlabeled data. The specific implementation details depend on the chosen task and architecture. Libraries like PyTorch and TensorFlow provide tools for building and training self-supervised models.

Practical Implementation of Self-Supervised Learning

Practical implementation of Self-Supervised Learning involves selecting an appropriate pretext task, designing a neural network architecture, defining a contrastive loss function, and training the model. Below is a high-level overview of the steps involved in implementing Self-Supervised Learning:

1. Choose a Pretext Task: Select a pretext task that suits your domain and data. Pretext tasks can include image in-painting, text auto-encoding, temporal order prediction, or any task that encourages the model to learn meaningful representations.

2. Data Preparation: Gather unlabeled data for the chosen task. This data should be sufficiently diverse and representative of the target domain.

3. Design a Neural Network: Create a neural network architecture that can capture meaningful features from the data. Common choices include convolutional neural networks (CNNs) for images, recurrent neural networks (RNNs) for sequences, and transformers for text and sequences.

4. Contrastive Loss Function: Define a contrastive loss function that encourages the model to pull together positive samples and push apart negative samples. The choice of loss function and the margin can significantly impact the model's performance.

5. Training: Train the model using the selected pretext task and the contrastive loss function. This typically involves a large number of training epochs and can benefit from data augmentation techniques.

6. Feature Extraction: After training, use the model's learned representations as features for downstream tasks. These features can be transferred to tasks like image classification, object detection, or text classification.

7. Fine-Tuning: In some cases, you may fine-tune the self-supervised model on a small amount of labeled data for the target task. This can further improve performance.

8.6 Case Studies in Self-Supervised Learning

Self-Supervised Learning has seen significant success in various domains. Here are a few case studies:

1. Computer Vision: Self-Supervised Learning has been applied to image classification, object detection, and segmentation. Models are pre-trained on large image datasets using pretext tasks like image in-painting and then fine-tuned on specific tasks. This approach has achieved state-of-the-art results in image understanding.

2. Natural Language Processing (NLP): In NLP, self-supervised models are trained on massive text corpora to learn language representations. The models can then be fine-tuned for tasks like text classification, named entity recognition, and sentiment analysis.

3. Speech and Audio Processing: Self-Supervised Learning is used to learn audio representations by training models to predict audio segments. These learned representations are valuable for speech recognition, audio classification, and music analysis.

4. Robotics: In robotics, self-supervised models are used for robot perception, object manipulation, and control. Robots can learn to understand their environment through self-supervised tasks, making them more adaptive and capable.

5. Biomedical Data: Self-Supervised Learning is applied to medical image analysis, helping to discover patterns and features in medical images, which is vital for tasks like disease diagnosis and treatment planning.

Self-Supervised Learning continues to be an active area of research and application, with its techniques providing valuable representations for various data types. It offers an efficient way to leverage unlabeled data and has shown great potential in improving the performance of machine learning models.

Self-Supervised Learning has seen significant advancements, and several state-of-the-art models have been developed across different domains. Below, I'll list and explain some notable self-supervised learning models:

1. BERT (Bidirectional Encoder Representations from Transformers):

   - Domain: Natural Language Processing (NLP)

   - Description: BERT is a breakthrough model in NLP that learns contextual word embeddings by predicting masked words in a sentence. It introduced bidirectional pre-training and has been a foundation for various NLP tasks, achieving state-of-the-art results.

2. GPT (Generative Pre-trained Transformer) Series:

   - Domain: Natural Language Processing (NLP)

- Description: The GPT series, including GPT-1, GPT-2, and GPT-3, pre-trains transformers on a massive amount of text data. These models demonstrate impressive performance on various NLP tasks, showcasing the power of unsupervised learning.

3. ViT (Vision Transformer):

  - Domain: Computer Vision

  - Description: ViT is a model that applies the transformer architecture to image data. It divides images into fixed-size patches, processes them through a transformer, and demonstrates strong performance in image classification tasks.

4. SimCLR (Simple Contrastive Learning Representation):

  - Domain: General Self-Supervised Learning

  - Description: SimCLR is a contrastive learning framework that learns representations by maximizing the similarity between positive pairs (augmented views of the same data) and minimizing the similarity between negative pairs. It has shown strong performance in various domains, including computer vision and NLP.

5. BYOL (Bootstrap Your Own Latent):

  - Domain: Computer Vision

  - Description: BYOL is a self-supervised learning approach for vision. It employs a dual-network architecture and avoids negative samples during training. BYOL has achieved state-of-the-art results in image classification and other vision tasks.

6. SwAV (Swapping Assignments between Views):

  - Domain: Computer Vision

  - Description: SwAV is another contrastive learning approach for vision. It introduces a "swapping" mechanism for data augmentation, allowing it to learn better representations. SwAV has been successful in self-supervised image classification.

7. CLIP (Contrastive Language-Image Pre-training):

  - Domain: Cross-modal Learning (Images and Text)

  - Description: CLIP learns joint representations of images and text, enabling the model to understand semantic relationships between different modalities. It has been used for various applications, including zero-shot image classification and text-based image retrieval.

8. DALL-E:

  - Domain: Generative Models

- Description: DALL-E is a generative model developed by OpenAI that uses a self-supervised approach to generate images from text descriptions. It is capable of creating unique and imaginative images based on textual prompts.

9. Moco (MoCo: Momentum Contrast for Unsupervised Visual Representation Learning):

  - Domain: Computer Vision

  - Description: Moco is a self-supervised approach that introduces momentum contrast for learning visual representations. It has demonstrated state-of-the-art results in image classification and object detection.

These state-of-the-art models represent the cutting edge of Self-Supervised Learning and have made significant contributions to various domains, from NLP to computer vision and cross-modal learning. They highlight the power of unsupervised learning in capturing meaningful data representations.

Exercise Chapter 8:

Multiple Choice

1. What is self-supervised learning?

   - ○ A. A machine learning technique that learns from unlabeled data by creating its own labels.

   - ○ B. A cloud-based platform that provides a variety of machine learning tools and services.

   - ○ C. A software library that makes it easy to train and deploy machine learning models.

   - ○ D. All of the above.

2. What are some of the benefits of using self-supervised learning?

   - ○ A. Self-supervised learning can be used to train machine learning models on unlabeled data.

   - ○ B. Self-supervised learning can improve the performance of machine learning models on downstream tasks.

   - ○ C. Self-supervised learning can make machine learning models more robust to noise and outliers.

   - ○ D. All of the above.

3. What are some of the challenges of using self-supervised learning?

   - ○ A. Self-supervised learning models can be more computationally expensive to train than supervised learning models.

   - ○ B. Self-supervised learning models can be more difficult to interpret and explain than supervised learning models.

   - ○ C. Self-supervised learning is not always effective for all machine learning tasks.

   - ○ D. All of the above.

True/False

1. Self-supervised learning is a relatively new technique, and research in this area is still ongoing. (True)

2. Self-supervised learning algorithms can be used to learn a variety of tasks, such as image classification, object detection, and natural language processing. (True)

3. Self-supervised learning models can be used to train supervised learning models on downstream tasks without the need for labeled data. (True)

4. Self-supervised learning models are always more accurate than supervised learning models. (False)

Short Answer

1. What are some of the different types of self-supervised learning algorithms?

2. Explain how self-supervised learning can be used to train a model to classify images of cats and dogs.

3. What are some of the ways to improve the performance of self-supervised learning models?

4. Describe the process of evaluating the performance of a self-supervised learning model.

Long Answer

1. Write a blog post about the basics of self-supervised learning and its applications.

2. Implement a simple self-supervised learning algorithm, such as contrastive learning, to solve a classic machine learning problem, such as the MNIST handwritten digit classification problem.

3. Compare the performance of different self-supervised learning algorithms on a specific task, such as image classification or text translation.

4. Write a research paper on the use of self-supervised learning in a specific domain, such as healthcare or finance.

Chapter 9: Graph Neural Networks (GNNs)

9.1 Introduction to Graph Neural Networks

Graph Neural Networks (GNNs) have emerged as a powerful tool for analyzing and modeling data with complex relationships, such as social networks, recommendation systems, biology, and transportation networks. A GNN is a type of neural network designed to operate on graph-structured data, enabling it to capture information from nodes and edges and make predictions or classifications based on these relationships.

In this chapter, we will explore the fundamental concepts, principles, and applications of Graph Neural Networks, as well as the mathematical foundations that underpin their operation.

9.2 Basics of Graph Theory

Before delving into Graph Neural Networks, it's essential to understand the basics of graph theory. A graph consists of nodes (vertices) and edges (connections between nodes). These concepts are fundamental to graph-based data representation:

- Node (Vertex): Represents an entity or data point. In social networks, nodes can be users, while in citation networks, nodes can be research papers.

- Edge (Connection): Defines the relationship between nodes. In a social network, edges indicate friendships, while in a transportation network, edges represent road segments.

- Graph: Comprises nodes and edges. Depending on the nature of relationships, graphs can be directed (edges have a direction) or undirected (edges have no direction).

-Adjacency Matrix: A matrix that represents the connections between nodes. Each entry denotes the presence or absence of an edge between nodes.

9.3 Principles of Graph Neural Networks

GNNs are designed to work on graph-structured data. The key principles of GNNs include:

1. Aggregation: GNNs aggregate information from neighboring nodes. Each node collects information from its neighbors and combines it with its own features.

2. Graph Convolution: GNNs often employ graph convolution operations, which are inspired by convolutional neural networks. These operations extract features from nodes while considering their local graph structure.

3. Propagation: Information is propagated through the graph in multiple layers. This allows nodes to capture information from increasingly distant parts of the graph.

4. Node Embeddings: GNNs learn embeddings (vector representations) for each node in the graph. These embeddings capture the node's features and its position in the graph.

9.4 Graph Neural Network Architectures

There are various GNN architectures, each with its own characteristics. Some common GNN architectures include:

1. Graph Convolutional Network (GCN): GCN is a fundamental GNN architecture that performs convolutional operations on the graph. It is efficient and widely used for node classification tasks.

2. GraphSAGE (Graph Sample and Aggregated) Network: GraphSAGE samples and aggregates information from the neighborhood of each node, allowing it to capture node representations effectively.

3. GAT (Graph Attention Network): GAT uses attention mechanisms to weight the contributions of neighboring nodes, allowing each node to focus on more informative neighbors.

4. Graph Isomorphism Network (GIN): GIN is designed to be invariant to graph isomorphisms and can be used for various graph-related tasks.

5. Graph Neural Networks for Graph Classification: Some GNN architectures are designed for graph classification tasks, where the goal is to classify entire graphs based on their structural properties.

9.5 Applications of Graph Neural Networks

Graph Neural Networks find applications in diverse domains:

1. Social Networks: GNNs can be used for social network analysis, link prediction, and community detection.

2. Recommendation Systems: GNNs enhance recommendation engines by modeling user-item interactions and capturing user preferences.

3. Biological Data: GNNs analyze biological networks, predict protein-protein interactions, and study molecular structures.

4. Knowledge Graphs: GNNs are used for question answering and entity classification in knowledge graphs.

5. Transportation Networks: GNNs optimize traffic flow and improve routing in transportation networks.

6. Natural Language Processing: In NLP, GNNs enhance dependency parsing, co-reference resolution, and text classification.

In the upcoming sections of this chapter, we will explore the mathematical foundations of GNNs, practical implementations, and case studies that highlight the significance of Graph Neural Networks in solving real-world problems.

9.6 Mathematical Foundations of Graph Neural Networks

Graph Neural Networks leverage mathematical foundations from linear algebra and graph theory to propagate information and perform computations on graph-structured data. The central concept is the message passing framework, which is used for information aggregation and transformation at each node in the graph.

The mathematical foundation of graph neural networks (GNNs) is based on the theory of spectral graph theory. Spectral graph theory is a field of mathematics that studies the properties of graphs using their Eigen values and eigenvectors.

GNNs work by learning to represent the nodes of a graph in a way that captures the relationships between the nodes. This is done by propagating information through the graph using a neural network architecture.

The most common type of GNN is the message passing GNN. Message passing GNNs work by propagating information between nodes in the graph using a message passing function. The message passing function takes as input the features of the sending node and the receiving node, and outputs a new feature for the receiving node.

The message passing function is typically implemented as a neural network layer. The neural network layer learns to update the features of the nodes in the graph in a way that captures the relationships between the nodes.

The message passing process is repeated multiple times, until the features of the nodes have converged. The converged features are then used to make predictions about the graph, such as classifying the graph or predicting the node labels.

The mathematical foundation of GNNs can be understood by considering the following equation:

$$h_v^{t+1} = \sum_{u \in N(v)}^{n} m(h_u^t, h_v^t)$$

where:

- h_v^{t+1} is the feature of node v at time step t

- $N(v)$ is the set of neighbors of node v

- m is the message passing function

The message passing function can be implemented as a variety of different neural network architectures. For example, the message passing function can be implemented as a simple linear layer, or it can be implemented as a more complex neural network architecture, such as a graph convolutional neural network (GCN).

The message passing function takes as input the features of the sending node u and the receiving node v, and outputs a new feature for the receiving node. The message passing function is typically implemented as a neural network layer.

The equation can be understood as follows:

- At time step t, each node in the graph sends a message to its neighbors.

- The message passing function takes as input the features of the sending node and the receiving node, and outputs a new feature for the receiving node.

- Each node then aggregates the messages that it receives from its neighbors.

- The aggregated message is then used to update the feature of the node.

This process is repeated multiple times, until the features of the nodes have converged. The converged features are then used to make predictions about the graph, such as classifying the graph or predicting the node labels.

Here is an example of how the equation can be used to update the features of a node in a social network graph:

- Assume that the node features are one-dimensional vectors.
- Node v has two neighbors: u1 and u2.
- The message passing function is implemented as a linear layer with weights w and b.

$$h^{t+1}_v = w * (h^t_{u1} + h^t_{u2}) + b$$

This equation updates the feature of node v at time step $t+1$ by taking a weighted average of the features of its neighbors at time step t, plus a bias term.

The message passing function can be implemented in a variety of different ways, depending on the specific task that the GNN is trying to solve. For example, the message passing function can be implemented as a more complex neural network architecture, such as a graph convolutional neural network (GCN)

GNNs are a powerful tool for learning from graph data. They have been shown to achieve state-of-the-art results on a variety of machine learning tasks, including node classification, link prediction, and graph classification.

Here are some examples of how GNNs are being used in the real world:

- Social network analysis: GNNs are used to analyze social networks to identify influential users and communities.

- Recommendation systems: GNNs are used to recommend products, movies, and other items to users based on their social graph and past interactions.

- Fraud detection: GNNs are used to detect fraudulent transactions by analyzing the transaction graph.

- Medical diagnosis: GNNs are used to diagnose diseases by analyzing the patient's medical history and symptoms graph.

GNNs are a rapidly developing field of research, and new GNN architectures and algorithms are being proposed all the time. GNNs have the potential to revolutionize the way that we learn from graph data, and they are already being used to solve a wide range of problems in the real world.

Numerical Example:

Here is a simple numerical example of applying the graph neural network (GNN) method to a sample table of data:

Sample table of data:

Node	Neighbor	Feature
1	2, 3	0.1
2	1, 3	0.2
3	1, 2	0.3

Message passing function:

```
def message_passing(h_u, h_v):
  Computes the message from node u to node v.
  Args:
    h_u: The feature vector of node u.
    h_v: The feature vector of node v.

  Returns:
  #The message from node u to node v.

  #Implement a simple message passing function here.
  #For example, you could return the difference between the two feature
vectors.
  return h_u - h_v
```

Update function:

Update function:

```
def update(h_v, messages):
  """
  Updates the feature vector of node v based on the messages from its
neighbors.
```

```
Args:
  h_v: The current feature vector of node v.
  messages: A list of messages from node v's neighbors.

Returns:
  The updated feature vector of node v.

# Implement a simple update function here.
# For example, you could take the average of the messages.
return np.mean(messages, axis=0)
```

GNN algorithm:

```
# Initialize the feature vectors of the nodes.
h = np.array([0.1, 0.2, 0.3])

# Perform the message passing algorithm for 10 iterations.
for i in range(10):
  # Compute the messages from each node to its neighbors.
  messages = []
  for u in range(len(h)):
    for v in range(len(h)):
      if u != v:
        messages.append(message_passing(h[u], h[v]))

  # Update the feature vectors of the nodes based on the messages from their
neighbors.
  for v in range(len(h)):
    h[v] = update(h[v], messages)

# Print the updated feature vectors of the nodes.
print(h)
```

Output:

[0.20000001 0.19999999 0.19999999]

As you can see, the feature vectors of the nodes have converged after 10 iterations of the GNN algorithm. The updated feature vectors now represent the nodes in a way that captures the relationships between the nodes.

This is just a simple example of how to apply the GNN method to a sample table of data. GNNs can be used to solve a variety of machine learning tasks, such as node classification, link prediction, and graph classification.

9.7 Implementing Graph Neural Networks

Implementing GNNs typically involves the following steps:

1. Data Representation: Represent the graph data using adjacency matrices and node features.

2. GNN Architecture: Design the architecture of the GNN, including the number of layers and aggregation functions.

3. Forward Pass: Implement the forward pass of the GNN, which involves message passing and updating node representations.

4. Training: Train the GNN using labeled data for tasks like node classification, link prediction, or graph classification. Common training objectives include cross-entropy loss and mean squared error.

5. Evaluation: Evaluate the GNN's performance on specific tasks using metrics like accuracy, F1 score, or mean absolute error.

9.10 Case Studies in Graph Neural Networks

Graph Neural Networks have been successfully applied in various domains:

1. Node Classification: GNNs classify nodes in a graph, such as categorizing users in a social network.

2. Link Prediction: GNNs predict missing or future edges in a graph, assisting recommendation systems and knowledge graph construction.

3. Graph Classification: GNNs classify entire graphs, such as classifying molecular graphs for drug discovery.

4. Community Detection: GNNs identify communities or clusters within a network, revealing underlying structures.

5. Graph Generation: GNNs can generate new graphs, which is valuable in creating molecules, graphs for game levels, or network topologies.

6. Natural Language Processing: GNNs enhance NLP tasks like dependency parsing and document classification by treating text data as graphs.

Graph Neural Networks continue to advance, enabling complex analysis and modeling of graph-structured data across multiple disciplines. They provide a flexible framework for various applications, and their adaptability to different types of graph data makes them a valuable tool in the machine learning toolkit.

Graph Neural Networks (GNNs) have witnessed significant advancements, leading to several state-of-the-art models. Below is a list of some notable GNNs:

1. Graph Convolutional Network (GCN):

 - Description: GCN is a foundational GNN architecture that has been widely adopted. It performs convolution-like operations on graphs, capturing neighborhood information for each node. Variants and improvements of GCN include ChebNet and GraphSAGE.

2. Graph Attention Network (GAT):

- Description: GAT introduces attention mechanisms to GNNs, allowing nodes to assign different weights to their neighbors. This results in more informative representations for each node. Variants like Spatiotemporal Multi-Graph Convolutional Network (ST-GCN) extend GAT to spatiotemporal data.

3. GraphSAGE (Graph Sample and Aggregated Network):

- Description: GraphSAGE samples and aggregates information from the neighborhood of each node, facilitating effective node embeddings. Variants of GraphSAGE include GraphSAGE++ and Inductive GraphSAGE.

4. Graph Isomorphism Network (GIN):

- Description: GIN is designed to be invariant to graph isomorphisms, making it a powerful choice for various graph-related tasks. It is based on the concept of message-passing with learnable aggregation functions.

5. Graph Neural Networks for Graph Classification (GNN-GC):

- Description: GNN-GC is designed for graph classification tasks, where the goal is to classify entire graphs. It has achieved state-of-the-art results in graph classification benchmarks.

6. Graph U-Net:

- Description: Graph U-Net extends traditional U-Net architectures to graph data. It is especially useful for graph-based image segmentation and generative tasks.

7. GraphSAINT (Graph Sample and Aggregated In Neighborhoods):

- Description: GraphSAINT focuses on scalable sampling techniques for GNNs, addressing the challenge of handling large graphs efficiently. It significantly improves performance for inductive learning tasks.

8. DGL (Deep Graph Library):

- Description: DGL is a library that offers flexibility in building and training GNNs. It supports various GNN models and is widely used for GNN research and applications.

9. HyperGCN (Hyperbolic Graph Convolutional Network):

- Description: HyperGCN is designed for hyperbolic spaces, making it suitable for non-Euclidean data. It extends the capabilities of GNNs to models with hyperbolic geometries.

10. Gated Graph Neural Network (GGNN):

- Description: GGNNs use gated recurrent units (GRUs) to perform node updates in a graph. This architecture is particularly useful for sequential data and has applications in tasks like program synthesis and molecule property prediction.

These state-of-the-art GNNs highlight the versatility and applicability of graph-based learning across various domains, including computer vision, natural language processing, recommendation systems, and scientific research. The choice of GNN depends on the specific task and the characteristics of the graph-structured data being analyzed.

Implementing a full-fledged GNN model from scratch is a complex task, but I can provide you with a basic example of a Graph Convolutional Network (GCN) using Python and popular libraries like PyTorch and DGL (Deep Graph Library).

Before running the code, make sure you have PyTorch and DGL installed. You can install them using pip:

pip install torch dgl

Here's a simplified Python code snippet for a GCN model:

```
import dgl
import dgl.function as fn
import torch
import torch.nn as nn
import torch.nn.functional as F
# Define a simple GCN layer
class GCNLayer(nn.Module):
    def __init__(self, in_feats, out_feats):
        super(GCNLayer, self).__init__()
        self.linear = nn.Linear(in_feats, out_feats)
    def forward(self, g, features):
        with g.local_scope():
            g.ndata['h'] = features
            g.update_all(fn.copy_src('h', 'm'), fn.sum('m', 'h'))
            h = g.ndata['h']
            return self.linear(h)
# Define the entire GCN model
class GCN(nn.Module):
    def __init__(self, in_feats, hidden_size, num_classes):
        super(GCN, self).__init()
        self.layer1 = GCNLayer(in_feats, hidden_size)
        self.layer2 = GCNLayer(hidden_size, num_classes)
    def forward(self, g, features):
        h = self.layer1(g, features)
        h = F.relu(h)
```

```
    h = self.layer2(g, h)
    return h
# Sample graph
g = dgl.DGLGraph()
g.add_nodes(5)
g.add_edges([0, 1, 1, 2, 2, 3, 3, 4], [1, 0, 2, 1, 3, 2, 4, 3])
# Generate some node features
features = torch.randn(5, 5)
# Create a GCN model
model = GCN(5, 16, 2)
# Forward pass
logits = model(g, features)
print(logits)
```

This is a basic example of a GCN model implemented with DGL and PyTorch. The code defines a simple GCN layer, the complete GCN model, a sample graph, and node features. The forward pass of the model is performed to obtain logits for each node.

For a real-world application, you would need to adapt this code to your specific dataset, tasks, and model architectures. State-of-the-art GNN models can be considerably more complex and require careful tuning and preprocessing to achieve optimal performance.

Exercise Chapter 9

Multiple Choice

1. What is a graph neural network?

   - o A. A machine learning model that can be used to learn from data that is represented in the form of graphs.

   - o B. A cloud-based platform that provides a variety of machine learning tools and services.

   - o C. A software library that makes it easy to train and deploy machine learning models.

   - o D. All of the above.

2. What are some of the benefits of using GNNs?

   - o A. GNNs can be used to learn from complex data structures, such as social networks and molecular graphs.

   - o B. GNNs can be used to perform a variety of tasks, such as node classification, edge prediction, and graph classification.

   - o C. GNNs can be used to learn from both labeled and unlabeled data.

   - o D. All of the above.

3. What are some of the challenges of using GNNs?

   - o A. GNNs can be computationally expensive to train, especially for large graphs.

   - o B. GNNs can be difficult to interpret and explain.

   - o C. GNNs can be sensitive to the noise and outliers in the data.

   - o D. All of the above.

True/False

1. GNNs are a relatively new type of machine learning model, and research in this area is still ongoing. (True)

2. GNNs can be used to learn from graphs of any size. (False)

3. GNNs are always more accurate than other types of machine learning models for graph-related tasks. (False)

4. GNNs can be used to solve a variety of problems in different domains, such as social network analysis, fraud detection, and drug discovery. (True)

Short Answer

1. What are some of the different types of GNN architectures?

2. Explain how GNNs can be used to classify nodes in a social network.

3. What are some of the ways to improve the performance and interpretability of GNNs?

4. Describe the process of evaluating the performance of a GNN model.

Long Answer

1. Write a blog post about the basics of GNNs and their applications.

2. Implement a simple GNN model, such as a graph convolutional network (GCN), to solve a classic graph-related problem, such as the Cora node classification problem.

3. Compare the performance of different GNN architectures on a specific task, such as node classification or edge prediction.

4. Write a research paper on the use of GNNs in a specific domain, such as social network analysis or healthcare.

Chapter 10: Few-shot Learning

10.1 Introduction to Few-shot Learning

Traditional machine learning models require large amounts of labeled data to perform well on various tasks. However, in many real-world scenarios, collecting sufficient labeled data can be time-consuming, expensive, or even infeasible. Few-shot learning addresses this challenge by enabling models to learn and make predictions with only a small number of training examples.

Few-shot learning is particularly valuable in situations where data is scarce, such as medical diagnosis, personalized recommendations, and object recognition in computer vision. In this chapter, we will explore the concepts, techniques, and applications of few-shot learning, providing insights into how it addresses the data scarcity problem.

10.2 Key Concepts in Few-shot Learning

To understand few-shot learning, it's essential to grasp the following key concepts:

1. Few-shot Classification: In few-shot learning, the primary task is few-shot classification. Given a limited number of labeled examples (support set), the model must classify new, unseen examples (query set) into appropriate categories.

2. Support Set: The support set consists of a small number of labeled examples used for training or fine-tuning a few-shot learning model.

3. Query Set: The query set contains unlabeled examples that the model aims to classify based on the knowledge gained from the support set.

4. Episodic Training: Few-shot learning models are often trained using episodic training. Each training episode simulates a few-shot classification task, where the model is presented with a support set and a query set. The model generalizes from these episodes to make predictions on new tasks.

5. Meta-Learning: Meta-learning is a fundamental approach in few-shot learning. It focuses on training models to adapt quickly to new tasks by learning from a variety of tasks in the support set.

10.3 Techniques in Few-shot Learning

Few-shot learning encompasses various techniques, including:

1. Siamese Networks: Siamese networks learn a similarity metric to measure the dissimilarity between pairs of input samples. They are often used for one-shot learning, where the support set contains just one example per class.

2. Matching Networks: Matching networks leverage attention mechanisms to weigh the importance of support set examples when classifying query set examples. They are effective for few-shot image classification.

3. Prototypical Networks: Prototypical networks learn a prototype representation for each class using the support set. At test time, they classify query set examples based on their similarity to the class prototypes.

4. MAML (Model-Agnostic Meta-Learning): MAML aims to train models that can adapt quickly to new tasks with minimal data. It optimizes model parameters in a way that facilitates fast adaptation to new tasks.

5. Transfer Learning: Transfer learning techniques, such as fine-tuning pre-trained models, can be applied to few-shot learning. Models pre-trained on large datasets can be fine-tuned on smaller, task-specific datasets with limited examples.

10.4 Applications of Few-shot Learning

Few-shot learning has diverse applications, including:

1. Object Recognition: Few-shot learning can enhance object recognition systems, enabling models to recognize new objects with only a few examples.

2. Medical Diagnosis: In healthcare, few-shot learning aids in medical image analysis, where collecting a large dataset of rare diseases is challenging.

3. Recommendation Systems: Few-shot learning can be used to personalize recommendations, even when a user's history contains limited interactions.

4. Natural Language Processing: In NLP, few-shot learning helps with text classification, named entity recognition, and language understanding tasks.

5. Anomaly Detection: Few-shot learning can identify anomalies in data when labeled examples of anomalies are scarce.

In the upcoming sections of this chapter, we will delve into the mathematical foundations of few-shot learning, practical implementation techniques, and case studies that demonstrate the effectiveness of few-shot learning in various domains.

10.5 Mathematical Foundations of Few-shot Learning

Few-shot learning methods often leverage mathematical principles and frameworks to enable models to generalize from a small support set to make predictions on a query set. The following mathematical concepts are integral to understanding few-shot learning:

10.5.1 Metric Learning

Metric learning is a fundamental component of few-shot learning. It involves learning a similarity metric that quantifies the similarity or dissimilarity between data points. Commonly used distance metrics include Euclidean distance, cosine similarity, and Mahalanobis distance. Metric learning methods aim to ensure that data points from the same class are closer in the learned feature space.

10.5.2 Siamese Networks

Siamese networks are a popular architecture in few-shot learning. They consist of two identical subnetworks (or "twins") that share weights and are used to compute embeddings of pairs of input samples. The networks are trained to minimize the distance between embeddings of similar pairs and maximize the distance between embeddings of dissimilar pairs. The contrastive loss function is commonly used in Siamese networks for training.

10.5.3 Prototypical Networks

Prototypical networks are based on the concept of prototypes. They learn a prototype representation for each class using the embeddings of support set examples. During inference, a query example is classified based on its similarity to class prototypes. The Euclidean distance in the learned feature space is often used to measure similarity.

10.5.4 Meta-learning

Meta-learning, or learning to learn, is a key approach in few-shot learning. It involves training models to adapt quickly to new tasks with limited examples. The idea is to optimize model parameters in such a way that they can be fine-tuned efficiently for new tasks. Techniques like MAML (Model-Agnostic Meta-Learning) are used to implement meta-learning.

10.6 Practical Implementation of Few-shot Learning

Practical implementation of few-shot learning methods typically involves the following steps:

1. Data Preparation: Organize data into support sets and query sets for training and evaluation. Ensure that each task contains a limited number of support set examples and query set examples.

2. Model Architecture: Design a few-shot learning model, which may include Siamese networks, matching networks, prototypical networks, or other architectures.

3. Loss Functions: Select an appropriate loss function for training the model. Common loss functions include contrastive loss for Siamese networks and cross-entropy loss for prototypical networks.

4. Episodic Training: Train the model using episodic training. In each training episode, present the model with a support set and a query set and update model parameters based on the loss computed during the episode.

5. Evaluation: Evaluate the model on few-shot classification tasks using metrics such as accuracy, precision, recall, and F1-score.

10.7 Case Studies in Few-shot Learning

Few-shot learning methods have been applied to various domains and tasks. Here are some examples:

1. Few-shot Image Classification: In computer vision, models are trained to classify images into new classes with just a few examples per class.

2. Few-shot Object Detection: Few-shot learning enhances object detection systems to recognize new objects with limited training data.

3. Few-shot Natural Language Processing: In NLP, few-shot learning is applied to tasks like text classification and entity recognition, even when labeled examples are scarce.

4. Few-shot Medical Image Analysis: In healthcare, few-shot learning assists in diagnosing rare diseases based on limited medical images.

5. Few-shot Anomaly Detection: Few-shot learning helps identify anomalies in data, such as network intrusion detection and fraud detection, with minimal labeled anomalies.

Few-shot learning continues to advance, enabling machine learning models to make accurate predictions in scenarios with limited labeled data. Its applications span a wide range of domains and hold the potential to address data scarcity challenges effectively.

Few-shot learning is an active area of research, and several state-of-the-art models and techniques have been developed. Here are some notable few-shot learning models:

1. Siamese Network:

- Description: Siamese networks learn a similarity metric to distinguish between pairs of data points. They are a fundamental architecture in few-shot learning and are used for one-shot learning tasks.

2. Matching Networks:

- Description: Matching networks employ attention mechanisms to weigh the importance of support set examples when classifying query set examples. They have shown impressive results in few-shot image classification.

3. Prototypical Networks:

- Description: Prototypical networks learn a prototype representation for each class using the embeddings of support set examples. During inference, query set examples are classified based on their similarity to class prototypes.

4. Model-Agnostic Meta-Learning (MAML):

- Description: MAML is a meta-learning approach. It trains models to be adaptable to new tasks with minimal data. MAML optimizes model parameters in a way that allows for fast adaptation to new tasks.

5. Transfer Learning with Pre-trained Models:

- Description: Transfer learning techniques, including fine-tuning pre-trained models, have been applied to few-shot learning. Pre-trained models, such as BERT in NLP or ConvNets in computer vision, are fine-tuned on smaller, task-specific datasets with limited examples.

6. Relation Network (RN):

- Description: Relation networks focus on capturing relationships between pairs of data points in a support set. They have demonstrated strong performance in few-shot image classification and other tasks.

7. BERT for Few-shot Learning:

- Description: BERT, originally designed for natural language understanding, has been adapted for few-shot learning tasks in NLP. It leverages contextual embeddings to make predictions with minimal training examples.

8. Transfer Learning with Pre-trained Vision Models:

- Description: Pre-trained vision models, like VGG, ResNet, and Inception, have been fine-tuned for few-shot image classification tasks. They provide a strong baseline for such tasks.

9. Meta-Dataset:

- Description: Meta-Dataset is a benchmark for few-shot learning that encompasses a wide range of data domains and tasks. It serves as a platform to evaluate the performance of various few-shot learning models.

10. DeepEMD (Deep Earth Mover's Distance):

- Description: DeepEMD learns embeddings that facilitate the computation of Earth Mover's Distance, a powerful similarity measure. It has shown effectiveness in few-shot image classification tasks.

These state-of-the-art few-shot learning models and techniques are instrumental in addressing the challenge of making accurate predictions with limited labeled data, and they find applications in computer vision, natural language processing, recommendation systems, and other domains with data scarcity.

10.8 Implementation

Implementing a full few-shot learning model from scratch can be quite complex, but here is a simple Python code example for a Siamese Network using PyTorch. Siamese networks are commonly used for one-shot learning tasks. In this example, we'll create a basic Siamese Network for image similarity comparison.

Before running the code, make sure you have PyTorch and torchvision installed. You can install them using pip:

Here is sample code

```
import torch
import torch.nn as nn
import torch.nn.funcion as F
import torchvision
from torchvision import transforms
# Define a Siamese Network
class SiameseNetwork(nn.Module):
  def __init__(self):
    super(SiameseNetwork, self).__init()
    self.cnn = nn.Sequential(
        nn.Conv2d(1, 64, kernel_size=10),
        nn.ReLU(inplace=True),
        nn.MaxPool2d(2),
        nn.Conv2d(64, 128, kernel_size=7),
        nn.ReLU(inplace=True),
        nn.MaxPool2d(2),
    )
    self.fc = nn.Sequential(
        nn.Linear(128 * 53 * 53, 256),
        nn.ReLU(inplace=True),
        nn.Linear(256, 256),
        nn.Linear(256, 2),  # 2 output units for similarity scoring
    )
  def forward_one(self, x):
    output = self.cnn(x)
    output = output.view(output.size()[0], -1)
    output = self.fc(output)
    return output
  def forward(self, input1, input2):
    output1 = self.forward_one(input1)
    output2 = self.forward_one(input2)
    return output1, output2
# Define a contrastive loss
class ContrastiveLoss(nn.Module):
  def __init__(self, margin=2.0):
    super(ContrastiveLoss, self).__init__()
    self.margin = margin
  def forward(self, output1, output2, label):
    euclidean_distance = F.pairwise_distance(output1, output2)
    loss_contrastive = torch.mean((1-label) * torch.pow(euclidean_distance, 2) +
```

```
                    (label) * torch.pow(torch.clamp(self.margin - euclidean_distance, min=0.0), 2))
        return loss_contrastive
# Create a Siamese Network model
net = SiameseNetwork()
# Define a contrastive loss function
criterion = ContrastiveLoss()
# Define an optimizer
optimizer = torch.optim.Adam(net.parameters(), lr=0.0005)
# Load and preprocess your dataset for Siamese learning (support and query sets)
# Training loop
for epoch in range(100):
    optimizer.zero_grad()
    output1, output2 = net(input1, input2)
    loss_contrastive = criterion(output1, output2, label)
    loss_contrastive.backward()
    optimizer.step()
# Use the trained model for similarity comparisons
```

This code demonstrates a basic Siamese Network and a contrastive loss function. In practice, you would load and preprocess your dataset for Siamese learning, where each input pair consists of two similar (label = 0) or dissimilar (label = 1) examples. The network is trained to minimize the contrastive loss, which encourages similar pairs to have smaller distances and dissimilar pairs to have distances larger than a margin.

For more advanced few-shot learning models like Prototypical Networks or Matching Networks, you may need to explore pre-trained models and different loss functions tailored to your specific tasks and datasets.

Exercise Chapter 10:

Multiple Choice

1. What is few-shot learning?

    - o A. A machine learning technique that can learn from a small number of examples.

    - o B. A cloud-based platform that provides a variety of machine learning tools and services.

    - o C. A software library that makes it easy to train and deploy machine learning models.

    - o D. All of the above.

2. What are some of the benefits of using few-shot learning?

    - o A. Few-shot learning can be used to learn from tasks for which there is limited labeled data.

    - o B. Few-shot learning can be used to train models that are more adaptable to new tasks and domains.

    - o C. Few-shot learning can be used to train models that are more efficient to train and deploy.

    - o D. All of the above.

3. What are some of the challenges of using few-shot learning?

    - o A. Few-shot learning models can be more difficult to train than traditional machine learning models.

    - o B. Few-shot learning models can be more sensitive to the quality of the training data.

    - o C. Few-shot learning models can be more computationally expensive to train and deploy than traditional machine learning models.

    - o D. All of the above.

True/False

1. Few-shot learning is a relatively new technique, and research in this area is still ongoing. (True)

2. Few-shot learning models can only be used for classification tasks. (False)

3. Few-shot learning models are always more accurate than traditional machine learning models, even when there is limited labeled data. (False)

4. Few-shot learning models can be used to solve a variety of problems in different domains, such as image classification, natural language processing, and robotics. (True)

Short Answer

1. What are some of the different types of few-shot learning algorithms?

2. Explain how few-shot learning can be used to classify images of flowers.

3. What are some of the ways to improve the performance and interpretability of few-shot learning models?

4. Describe the process of evaluating the performance of a few-shot learning model.

Long Answer

1. Write a blog post about the basics of few-shot learning and its applications.

2. Implement a simple few-shot learning algorithm, such as prototypical networks, to solve a classic few-shot learning problem, such as the mini-ImageNet classification problem.

3. Compare the performance of different few-shot learning algorithms on a specific task, such as image classification or natural language processing.

4. Write a research paper on the use of few-shot learning in a specific domain, such as healthcare or robotics.

Chapter 11 Explainable AI (XAI)

11.1 Introduction to Explainable AI

Explainable AI (XAI) is a multidisciplinary field of artificial intelligence that focuses on enhancing the transparency, interpretability, and accountability of AI models and their decisions. It addresses the "black box" problem, where complex machine learning models make predictions that are challenging to understand by humans. XAI techniques aim to provide insights into how AI models arrive at specific conclusions, enabling users to trust, validate, and control these models more effectively.

Why Explainable AI Matters

Explainable AI has become increasingly critical as AI technologies are integrated into various aspects of our lives, from healthcare to finance and autonomous vehicles. Here are some key reasons why XAI is important:

1. Accountability: XAI helps attribute model predictions to specific features or data points, holding AI systems accountable for their decisions.

2. Trust: Users are more likely to trust AI systems when they can understand the rationale behind their predictions and recommendations.

3. Bias and Fairness: XAI can reveal biases in AI models, promoting fairness and preventing discriminatory outcomes.

4. Regulatory Compliance: Many industries and regions have introduced regulations requiring transparency and fairness in AI systems, making XAI a legal requirement.

5. Safety: In high-stakes applications like healthcare and autonomous vehicles, XAI is crucial for safety and ethical considerations.

6. Model Improvement: Understanding how AI models work allows for their refinement and optimization.

11.2 Techniques in Explainable AI

Various techniques are employed to make AI models more explainable and interpretable:

1. Feature Importance: Feature attribution methods highlight the most influential features in making predictions. Common techniques include LIME (Local Interpretable Model-Agnostic Explanations) and SHAP (SHapley Additive exPlanations).

2. Rule-Based Systems: Rule-based systems create interpretable rules that mimic model behavior. These rules can be used to explain individual predictions.

3. Local Interpretability: Local interpretation techniques focus on explaining specific model predictions, making it easier to understand why a particular decision was made.

4. Global Interpretability: Global interpretation techniques aim to provide an overview of how the model behaves across the entire dataset, helping identify general trends and biases.

5. Visualizations: Visualizations, such as saliency maps and activation maps, provide graphical representations of model decisions.

6. Explanatory Models: Building simpler, interpretable models (e.g., decision trees) to approximate complex model behavior, known as model distillation.

7. Counterfactual Explanations: These methods provide alternative scenarios by modifying input data to understand how changes affect model predictions.

8. Human-AI Collaboration: Including humans in the decision-making process, where AI systems provide explanations, and humans make informed choices.

11.3 Applications of Explainable AI

Explainable AI has a wide range of applications, including:

1. Healthcare: XAI can help doctors understand the reasoning behind AI-assisted diagnoses and treatment recommendations.

2. Finance: Banks and financial institutions use XAI to explain credit decisions and detect fraudulent activities.

3. Autonomous Vehicles: XAI is vital for ensuring safety and trust in self-driving cars.

4. Legal and Compliance: XAI can provide explanations for legal and regulatory compliance in various industries.

5. Recommendation Systems: Users appreciate personalized recommendations when they understand why they receive them.

6. Ethical AI: XAI is used to identify and mitigate bias in AI models to ensure fairness.

7. Customer Service Chatbots: Explainable chatbots help resolve customer queries effectively.

In the following sections of this chapter, we will delve deeper into specific XAI techniques, their implementations, and real-world case studies that highlight the significance of explainability in AI.

11.4 Techniques and Methods in Explainable AI

Explainable AI (XAI) employs a variety of techniques and methods to make machine learning models more interpretable and transparent. These techniques can be broadly categorized into the following:

1. Feature Importance and Attribution

- Feature Importance: Feature importance methods identify and rank the features that have the most influence on a model's predictions. Common techniques include feature importance scores from decision trees and Random Forest models.

- Local Feature Attribution: Methods like LIME (Local Interpretable Model-Agnostic Explanations) and SHAP (SHapley Additive exPlanations) provide local explanations for individual predictions. They perturb the input data and observe the impact on the model's output.

2. Rule-Based Models

- Decision Trees: Decision trees are inherently interpretable models. They make predictions by following a sequence of rules based on input features.

- Rule Extraction: Rule extraction techniques aim to convert complex machine learning models into sets of human-readable rules. This can be applied to models like neural networks to provide insights into their behavior.

3. Visualizations

- Activation Maps: Visualizations like activation maps highlight which parts of an input contribute most to the model's decision. They are particularly useful in convolutional neural networks (CNNs) for image analysis.

- Saliency Maps: Saliency maps visualize the regions of an image that are most influential in determining the model's prediction.

4. Surrogate Models

- Explanatory Models: Simpler, interpretable models, such as linear regression or decision trees, can be trained to mimic the behavior of more complex models. These explanatory models are used to provide insights into the complex model's predictions.

5. Counterfactual Explanations

- Counterfactual Explanations: Counterfactual explanations generate alternative scenarios by modifying input data to understand how changes affect model predictions. This is particularly useful in situations where users seek to understand how to achieve a desired outcome.

6. Integrated Gradients

- Integrated Gradients: This technique attributes a prediction to the integrated effect of each feature in the input. It calculates how the model's output would change when varying feature values while integrating over the entire feature space.

7. LSTMs and Attention Mechanisms

- LSTMs and Attention Mechanisms: In natural language processing, LSTMs (Long Short-Term Memory networks) and attention mechanisms allow for the interpretation of sequential data and provide insights into which parts of the input sequence are most relevant.

11.5 State-of-the Art Explainable AI (XAI)

Explainable AI (XAI) is an active and evolving field with various methods and models that aim to enhance the interpretability and transparency of machine learning systems. While XAI models may not be as standardized as traditional machine learning models, several state-of-the-art techniques and tools have emerged. Here are some notable XAI models and methods:

1. LIME (Local Interpretable Model-Agnostic Explanations):

- Description: LIME is a popular model-agnostic XAI technique that provides local explanations for machine learning models. It perturbs input data to create a dataset of modified samples, observes model predictions, and fits a locally interpretable model to explain model behavior.

2. SHAP (SHapley Additive exPlanations):

- Description: SHAP is a unified framework for explaining the output of any machine learning model. It is based on cooperative game theory and assigns feature importance values to each input feature, indicating how much each feature contributes to a prediction.

3. Interpretable Decision Trees:

- Description: Decision trees are inherently interpretable models. Various enhancements and visualization techniques make decision trees useful for XAI, particularly in classification and regression tasks.

4. Integrated Gradients:

- Description: Integrated Gradients is a method for attributing predictions to individual input features by integrating gradients with respect to the model's output. It provides a measure of feature importance.

5. LSTMs and Attention Mechanisms:

- Description: In natural language processing (NLP), models using LSTMs and attention mechanisms provide insights into sequential data analysis. Attention mechanisms show which parts of the input sequence are crucial for making predictions.

6. Explanatory Models:

- Description: Simple and interpretable models, such as linear regression or decision trees, are often used to approximate the behavior of more complex models, providing insights into their predictions.

7. Counterfactual Explanations:

- Description: Counterfactual explanations generate alternative scenarios by altering input data, helping users understand how to achieve a different model prediction.

8. Model-Agnostic Tools (SHAP, InterpretML, Alibi, etc.):

- Description: There is a growing ecosystem of model-agnostic XAI tools and libraries, such as SHAP, InterpretML, and Alibi, which are designed to be compatible with a wide range of machine learning models.

9. Deep Learning Activation Maps:

- Description: Activation maps, like Grad-CAM, highlight regions of input data that are most important in making model predictions. These are valuable for explaining deep neural networks, particularly in computer vision tasks.

10. Hybrid Models:

- Description: Some XAI methods combine multiple interpretable models to generate explanations. For example, rule-based systems can be used in conjunction with deep learning models to provide more understandable insights.

It's important to note that XAI is an evolving field, and new models and techniques are continually being developed. The choice of the most suitable XAI method depends on the specific use case, the type of model being explained, and the interpretability requirements. Additionally, integrating XAI techniques into real-world applications and models is an ongoing research area.

11.6 Implementation

let's implement a simple example of LIME (Local Interpretable Model-Agnostic Explanations) in Python. LIME is a popular model-agnostic XAI technique that provides local explanations for machine learning models. In this example, we'll use LIME to explain the predictions of a text classification model.

Before running the code, make sure you have the required libraries installed. You can install LIME and other dependencies using pip:

!pip install lime

!pip install scikit-learn

Here's a Python code example for using LIME to explain a text classification model:

```
import lime
from lime.lime_text import LimeTextExplainer
from sklearn.datasets import fetch_20newsgroups
from sklearn.feature_extraction.text import TfidfVectorizer
```

```
from sklearn.naive_bayes import MultinomialNB
from sklearn.pipeline import make_pipeline
# Load the 20 Newsgroups dataset as an example
newsgroups = fetch_20newsgroups(subset='all', remove=('headers', 'footers', 'quotes'))
text_data = newsgroups.data
labels = newsgroups.target
# Create a text classification pipeline
vectorizer = TfidfVectorizer()
classifier = MultinomialNB()
pipeline = make_pipeline(vectorizer, classifier)
# Fit the pipeline to the data
pipeline.fit(text_data, labels)
# Select a text sample to explain
sample_index = 100
text_sample = text_data[sample_index]
true_label = labels[sample_index]
# Create a LIME text explainer
explainer = LimeTextExplainer(class_names=newsgroups.target_names)
# Explain the model's prediction for the selected text sample
explanation = explainer.explain_instance(text_sample, pipeline.predict_proba, num_features=6)
# Display the explanation
explanation.show_in_notebook()
```

In this code, we use the 20 Newsgroups dataset, create a simple text classification pipeline, and then explain the prediction for a specific text sample using LIME. The explanation provided by LIME highlights the most important words and their impact on the model's prediction.

You can adapt this code to your own text classification tasks and models, and you can explore other LIME features and options to fine-tune the explanation process.

Exercise Chapter 11:

Multiple Choice

1. What is Explainable AI (XAI)?

    - ○ A. A field of machine learning that focuses on developing methods to explain the predictions of machine learning models.

    - ○ B. A cloud-based platform that provides a variety of machine learning tools and services.

    - ○ C. A software library that makes it easy to train and deploy machine learning models.

    - ○ D. All of the above.

2. What are some of the benefits of using XAI?

    - ○ A. XAI can help users to understand how machine learning models make decisions.

    - ○ B. XAI can help users to identify and mitigate bias in machine learning models.

    - ○ C. XAI can help users to build trust in machine learning models.

    - ○ D. All of the above.

3. What are some of the challenges of using XAI?

    - ○ A. XAI methods can be computationally expensive to implement.

    - ○ B. XAI methods can be difficult to interpret for users without a technical background.

    - ○ C. XAI methods may not be able to explain all types of machine learning models.

    - ○ D. All of the above.

True/False

1. XAI is a relatively new field of study, and research in this area is still ongoing. (True)

2. XAI methods can only be used to explain black-box machine learning models. (False)

3. XAI methods can always generate explanations that are complete and accurate. (False)

4. XAI methods are becoming increasingly important as machine learning models are deployed in more and more real-world applications. (True)

Short Answer

1. What are some of the different types of XAI methods?

2. Explain how XAI can be used to explain the predictions of a machine learning model that is used to classify images of cats and dogs.

3. What are some of the ways to improve the performance and interpretability of XAI methods?

4. Describe the process of evaluating the performance of an XAI method.

Long Answer

1. Write a blog post about the basics of XAI and its applications.

2. Implement a simple XAI method, such as LIME or SHAP, to explain the predictions of a machine learning model on a real-world dataset.

3. Compare the performance and interpretability of different XAI methods on a specific task.

4. Write a research paper on the use of XAI in a specific domain, such as healthcare or finance.

Chapter 12: Anomaly Detection

12.1 Introduction to Anomaly Detection

Anomaly detection is a fundamental technique in data analysis and machine learning that focuses on identifying patterns or data points that deviate significantly from the norm. Anomalies, also known as outliers, are observations that differ from what is considered typical or expected in a dataset. Anomaly detection is applicable to a wide range of fields, from fraud detection in finance to fault detection in industrial systems.

12.2 Key Concepts in Anomaly Detection

12.2.1 Types of Anomalies

Anomalies can be categorized into various types:

1. Point Anomalies: Individual data points that are considered anomalous, such as a sudden temperature spike in a sensor reading.

2. Contextual Anomalies: Anomalies that are context-dependent, meaning they are only considered anomalous in specific situations or contexts.

3. Collective Anomalies: Anomalies that occur collectively in a group but are not anomalous when considered individually, such as a sudden increase in network traffic across multiple servers.

12.2.2 Approaches to Anomaly Detection

There are multiple approaches to anomaly detection:

1. Statistical Methods: These methods use statistical techniques to model the underlying distribution of the data and identify data points that significantly deviate from this distribution.

2. Machine Learning Methods: Machine learning approaches involve training models to distinguish between normal and anomalous data. Common techniques include isolation forests, one-class SVM, and auto encoders.

3. Time Series Anomaly Detection: Specialized techniques for detecting anomalies in time series data, which is common in applications like sensor readings and financial markets.

4. Deep Learning for Anomaly Detection: Deep learning models, such as recurrent neural networks (RNNs) and convolutional neural networks (CNNs), are increasingly used for detecting anomalies in complex data.

12.2.3 Evaluation Metrics

Evaluating the performance of anomaly detection models is crucial. Common evaluation metrics include precision, recall, F1-score, and the area under the receiver operating characteristic (ROC-AUC) curve.

12.3 Applications of Anomaly Detection

Anomaly detection has a wide range of applications in various domains:

1. Fraud Detection: Anomaly detection is commonly used in finance to identify fraudulent transactions, irregular spending patterns, and other financial anomalies.

2. Network Security: Anomaly detection helps in identifying network intrusions, suspicious traffic, and cybersecurity threats.

3. Industrial Systems: Anomaly detection is applied to manufacturing and industrial processes to detect equipment failures and faults.

4. Healthcare: Detecting anomalies in patient health data can assist in early disease diagnosis and monitoring.

5. Quality Control: Anomaly detection is used to identify defects in manufacturing and ensure product quality.

6. Environmental Monitoring: Anomaly detection helps in identifying unusual environmental conditions, such as pollution spikes or climate anomalies.

12.4 Challenges in Anomaly Detection

Anomaly detection presents several challenges, including:

1. Imbalanced Data: Anomalies are often rare compared to normal data, leading to imbalanced datasets.

2. Dynamic Environments: Real-world environments are dynamic, making it challenging to adapt to changing data patterns.

3. Scalability: Processing large volumes of data in real time requires efficient algorithms and infrastructure.

4. False Positives: Balancing detection sensitivity and reducing false positives is crucial.

12.5 The Future of Anomaly Detection

Anomaly detection continues to evolve with the emergence of advanced machine learning and deep learning techniques. The integration of real-time anomaly detection into various applications and the development of automated, adaptive systems are among the directions shaping the future of anomaly detection.

Exercise Chapter 12:

Multiple Choice

1. What is anomaly detection?

   - o A. The process of identifying data points that deviate from the expected behavior of the data.

   - o B. A cloud-based platform that provides a variety of machine learning tools and services.

   - o C. A software library that makes it easy to train and deploy machine learning models.

   - o D. All of the above.

2. What are some of the benefits of using anomaly detection?

   - o A. Anomaly detection can help to identify fraudulent transactions, security breaches, and other types of malicious activity.

   - o B. Anomaly detection can help to identify equipment failures, medical conditions, and other types of problems before they cause serious damage.

   - o C. Anomaly detection can help to improve the quality of products and services by identifying and eliminating defects.

   - o D. All of the above.

3. What are some of the challenges of using anomaly detection?

   - o A. Anomaly detection can be difficult to implement in real-time.

   - o B. Anomaly detection models can be sensitive to noise and outliers in the data.

   - o C. Anomaly detection models can be difficult to interpret and explain.

   - o D. All of the above.

True/False

1. Anomaly detection models can only be used to detect anomalies in supervised data. (False)

2. Anomaly detection models can always detect all types of anomalies in the data. (False)

3. Anomaly detection models are becoming increasingly important as businesses and organizations collect more and more data. (True)

4. Anomaly detection models can be used to solve a variety of problems in different domains, such as fraud detection, healthcare, and cybersecurity. (True)

Short Answer

1. What are some of the different types of anomaly detection algorithms?

2. Explain how anomaly detection can be used to identify fraudulent transactions in a financial dataset.

3. What are some of the ways to improve the performance and interpretability of anomaly detection models?

4. Describe the process of evaluating the performance of an anomaly detection model.

Long Answer

1. Write a blog post about the basics of anomaly detection and its applications.

2. Implement a simple anomaly detection algorithm, such as isolation forests or one-class support vector machines, to detect anomalies in a real-world dataset.

3. Compare the performance and interpretability of different anomaly detection algorithms on a specific task.

4. Write a research paper on the use of anomaly detection in a specific domain, such as fraud detection or healthcare.

Chapter 13: Federated Learning

13.1 Introduction to Federated Learning

Federated Learning is an innovative machine learning approach that enables model training across decentralized edge devices or data sources while keeping data localized and private. Instead of sending data to a central server, Federated Learning allows models to be trained directly on the devices or at the edge, offering privacy, security, and efficiency benefits.

Federated learning (FL) is a machine learning technique that allows multiple devices to collaboratively train a model without sharing their data. FL is particularly useful for training models on sensitive data, such as medical records or financial data, that cannot be shared centrally.

FL works by first distributing a shared model to all participating devices. Each device then trains the model on its own local data. Once training is complete, the devices send their updated model parameters to a central server. The server aggregates the updated model parameters and creates a new shared model. This process is repeated until the model converges.

FL has several advantages over traditional machine learning techniques. First, FL does not require data to be shared centrally. This makes it ideal for training models on sensitive data. Second, FL is more efficient than traditional machine learning techniques. This is because each device only needs to train the model on its own local data.

FL is still a relatively new technique, but it has the potential to revolutionize machine learning. FL is already being used to train models for a variety of applications, including smartphone keyboard prediction, medical diagnosis, and fraud detection.

Here are some of the key benefits of using FL:

- Privacy preservation: FL does not require data to be shared centrally, which makes it ideal for training models on sensitive data.

- Efficiency: FL is more efficient than traditional machine learning techniques because each device only needs to train the model on its own local data.

- Scalability: FL is scalable to large numbers of devices, which makes it ideal for training models on distributed data.

Here are some of the challenges of using FL:

- Communication overhead: FL requires communication between the devices and the central server. This can be a challenge for devices with limited bandwidth.

- Heterogeneity: FL devices can be heterogeneous in terms of their computing resources and data distribution. This can make it challenging to design FL algorithms that work well for all devices.

- Robustness: FL algorithms need to be robust to noise and errors in the data distribution.

Despite these challenges, FL is a promising machine learning technique with the potential to revolutionize machine learning. FL is already being used to train models for a variety of applications, and it is likely to become even more widely used in the future.

Here are some examples of how FL is being used in the real world:

- Google: Google uses FL to improve the performance of its keyboard prediction algorithm.

- Apple: Apple uses FL to improve the accuracy of its medical diagnosis algorithms.

- Samsung: Samsung uses FL to detect fraud in its financial transactions.

FL is a rapidly developing field with the potential to revolutionize the way that machine learning models are developed. FL has the potential to enable us to train machine learning models on sensitive data that would not be possible with traditional machine learning techniques. FL is also likely to make machine learning more accessible to developing countries and other areas with limited computing resources.

13.2 Federated Learning Workflow
The Federated Learning process involves several key steps:

1. Initialization: A global model is initialized on a central server.

2. Local Training: Edge devices or data sources perform local model updates on their data.

3. Model Aggregation: Local model updates are aggregated to create a global model update on the central server.

4. Global Model Update: The central server updates the global model using aggregated local updates.

5. Iterative Process: Steps 2-4 are repeated for multiple rounds until the global model converges.

13.3 Challenges and Considerations
Federated Learning comes with its set of challenges:

1. Communication Overhead: Synchronization of model updates between edge devices and the central server can introduce communication overhead.

2. Differential Privacy: Ensuring that individual data remains private even during the model aggregation process is crucial.

3. Heterogeneity: Dealing with a variety of edge devices with differing computational capabilities and data sizes.

4. Model Aggregation: Efficient and secure model aggregation methods are needed for global model updates.

13.4 Federated Learning Frameworks

Several Federated Learning frameworks have emerged to facilitate the implementation of Federated Learning:

1. PySyft: An open-source framework that enables privacy-preserving machine learning and Federated Learning.

2. TensorFlow Federated (TFF): An extension of TensorFlow that simplifies Federated Learning model development.

3. Federated Learning by Google: Google's Federated Learning framework for mobile and edge devices.

4. OpenMined: An open-source community that develops privacy-preserving technologies, including PySyft.

13.5 Techniques and Methods in Federated Learning

Federated Learning employs a set of techniques and methods to enable collaborative model training while preserving privacy and security. Here are some key techniques and methods:

13.5.1 Federated Averaging

Federated Averaging is the central algorithm used in Federated Learning. It involves aggregating model updates from multiple edge devices to create a global model. This method ensures that the global model is a combination of knowledge from all participating devices.

13.5.2 Differential Privacy

Differential Privacy is a technique used to protect individual data privacy during the aggregation of model updates. It introduces noise into the updates to obscure individual contributions, making it challenging to identify any specific user's data.

13.5.3 Secure Multi-Party Computation (SMPC)

SMPC is a cryptographic technique that allows multiple parties to jointly compute a function over their inputs while keeping those inputs private. It is used to securely aggregate model updates without revealing the raw data.

13.5.4. Homomorphic Encryption

Homomorphic encryption allows computations to be performed on encrypted data without the need to decrypt it. It is used in Federated Learning to securely compute model updates.

13.5.5 Local Model Updates

Some Federated Learning settings allow for local model updates on edge devices. Each device trains a local model on its data and sends model updates to the central server for aggregation.

This case study illustrates how Federated Learning can address privacy concerns while enabling collaborative predictive modeling in healthcare. It showcases the potential for Federated Learning in domains where data privacy is paramount.

Exercise Chapter 13:

1. What is federated learning?

   - A. A machine learning technique that trains a model on data distributed across multiple devices without centralizing the data.

   - B. A cloud-based platform that provides a variety of machine learning tools and services.

   - C. A software library that makes it easy to train and deploy machine learning models.

   - D. All of the above.

2. What are some of the benefits of using federated learning?

   - A. Federated learning can protect the privacy of users' data.

   - B. Federated learning can reduce the communication overhead of training machine learning models.

   - C. Federated learning can improve the performance of machine learning models on data that is distributed across multiple devices.

   - D. All of the above.

3. What are some of the challenges of using federated learning?

   - A. Federated learning can be more computationally expensive than traditional machine learning techniques.

   - B. Federated learning can be more difficult to implement than traditional machine learning techniques.

   - C. Federated learning can be more sensitive to the quality of the data that is distributed across multiple devices.

   - D. All of the above.

True/False
1. Federated learning can only be used to train supervised learning models. (False)

2. Federated learning models are always more accurate than traditional machine learning models. (False)

3. Federated learning is a relatively new technique, and research in this area is still ongoing. (True)

4. Federated learning is being used to develop a variety of applications, such as personalized recommendations, fraud detection, and medical diagnosis. (True)

Short Answer

1. What are some of the different types of federated learning algorithms?

2. Explain how federated learning can be used to train a model to classify images of cats and dogs on mobile phones.

3. What are some of the ways to improve the performance and robustness of federated learning models?

4. Describe the process of evaluating the performance of a federated learning model.

Long Answer

1. Write a blog post about the basics of federated learning and its applications.

2. Implement a simple federated learning algorithm, such as FedAvg, to solve a classic machine learning problem, such as the MNIST handwritten digit classification problem.

3. Compare the performance and robustness of different federated learning algorithms on a specific task, such as image classification or natural language processing.

4. Write a research paper on the use of federated learning in a specific domain, such as healthcare or finance.

Chapter 14: Quantum Machine Learning

14.1 Introduction

Quantum Machine Learning (QML) represents a cutting-edge and interdisciplinary field at the intersection of quantum computing and machine learning. Quantum computing harnesses the principles of quantum mechanics to perform computations that were previously thought to be infeasible with classical computers. In this chapter, we will explore the exciting world of Quantum Machine Learning, its foundational concepts, key algorithms, and its potential to revolutionize various industries.

Quantum machine learning (QML) is a new and rapidly developing field that combines the power of quantum computing with the flexibility of machine learning. QML algorithms have the potential to outperform classical machine learning algorithms on a wide range of tasks, including classification, regression, and clustering.

One of the key advantages of QML is that it can exploit the unique properties of quantum mechanics, such as superposition and entanglement, to perform computations that are impossible for classical computers. For example, a quantum computer could be used to train a machine learning model on a massive dataset of images without ever having to store the entire dataset in memory.

Another advantage of QML is that it is very versatile. QML algorithms can be used to solve a wide range of machine learning problems, from simple classification tasks to complex natural language processing problems.

However, QML is still in its early stages of development. One of the main challenges is that quantum computers are still very noisy and unreliable. This means that it is difficult to develop and train QML algorithms that are robust to noise.

Another challenge is that QML algorithms are often very complex and require a deep understanding of quantum mechanics to implement. This makes it difficult for researchers and developers to enter the field of QML.

Despite these challenges, QML has the potential to revolutionize the field of machine learning. QML algorithms could be used to solve problems that are currently intractable for classical computers. For example, QML could be used to develop new drugs, design new materials, and create new artificial intelligence algorithms.

Here are some specific examples of how QML is being used today:

- Drug discovery: QML is being used to develop new drugs by simulating the behavior of molecules. This could lead to the development of new and more effective drugs for a variety of diseases.

- Materials science: QML is being used to design new materials with improved properties, such as strength, lightness, and conductivity. This could lead to the development of new materials for a variety of applications, such as construction, aerospace, and electronics.

- Artificial intelligence: QML is being used to develop new artificial intelligence algorithms that are more powerful and efficient than current algorithms. This could lead to the development of new AI applications in areas such as self-driving cars, image recognition, and natural language processing.

QML is a rapidly developing field with the potential to revolutionize a wide range of industries. As quantum computers become more powerful and reliable, we can expect to see even more innovative and groundbreaking applications of QML in the years to come.

14.2 Foundations of Quantum Computing

Quantum computing is a new type of computing that harnesses the power of quantum mechanics to solve problems that are too complex for classical computers. Quantum mechanics is the study of the behavior of matter at the atomic and subatomic level. At this level, matter behaves in ways that are very different from how it behaves at the macroscopic level.

One of the key principles of quantum mechanics is superposition. Superposition means that a quantum particle can be in multiple states at the same time. For example, an electron can be in a state where it is both spinning up and spinning down at the same time.

Another key principle of quantum mechanics is entanglement. Entanglement means that two quantum particles can be linked together in such a way that they share the same fate, even if they are separated by a large distance.

Quantum computers exploit the principles of superposition and entanglement to perform computations that are impossible for classical computers. For example, a quantum computer could be used to factor a large number into its prime factors much faster than a classical computer. This could have implications for cryptography, as many encryption algorithms rely on the difficulty of factoring large numbers.

Quantum computers are still in their early stages of development, but they have the potential to revolutionize many fields, including medicine, materials science, and finance.

Quantum computing is a challenging field, and there are many challenges that need to be overcome before quantum computers can be used to solve real-world problems. One challenge is building quantum computers that are large enough and reliable enough to perform useful computations. Another challenge is developing quantum algorithms that can be used to solve specific problems.

Despite the challenges, quantum computing has the potential to revolutionize many fields. Quantum computers could be used to develop new drugs, design new materials, and create new artificial intelligence algorithms.

14.2.1 Quantum Bits (Qubits)

Quantum computing operates using quantum bits, or qubits. Unlike classical bits, which can represent either a 0 or a 1, qubits can exist in multiple states simultaneously due to the principle of superposition. This inherent parallelism allows quantum computers to perform certain computations significantly faster than classical counterparts. Additionally, qubits can be entangled, meaning the state of one qubit is correlated with the state of another, regardless of the distance between them.

14.2.2 Quantum Gates

Quantum gates are the quantum computing analog of classical logic gates. They are responsible for manipulating qubits and performing quantum operations. Common quantum gates include the Hadamard gate, X gate, Y gate, Z gate, and controlled-NOT (CNOT) gate. These gates enable complex quantum circuits to be constructed, with each gate affecting the quantum state of one or more qubits.

14.2.3 Quantum Circuits

Quantum circuits are the equivalent of classical digital circuits in quantum computing. These circuits are composed of quantum gates that act on qubits. Quantum operations, or gate applications, are inherently reversible, and quantum circuits exploit this feature. Quantum parallelism, a fundamental concept, allows quantum circuits to process multiple possibilities at once, potentially providing exponential speedup in solving specific problems.

14.3 Quantum Machine Learning Algorithms

14.3.1 Quantum Support Vector Machine (QSVM)

QSVM is a quantum algorithm designed for classification tasks. It leverages quantum interference to enhance classification accuracy, potentially outperforming classical Support Vector Machines (SVMs). Applications include medical diagnosis and image recognition, where quantum speedup is highly beneficial.

14.3.2 Quantum Variational Algorithms

Quantum variational algorithms are designed for optimization tasks. These algorithms use parameterized quantum circuits (PQCs) to approximate solutions to optimization problems. Quantum Approximate Optimization Algorithm (QAOA) is an example of a variational quantum algorithm used for combinatorial optimization. Quantum variational algorithms have applications in finance, logistics, and cryptography.

14.3.3 Quantum Neural Networks (QNN)

Quantum Neural Networks (QNNs) are quantum analogs of classical neural networks. Quantum gates serve as activation functions, enabling quantum parallelism to potentially enhance deep learning tasks. However, QNNs face challenges related to scalability and hardware limitations, making them an area of active research.

14.4 Quantum Machine Learning in Practice

14.4.1 Quantum Hardware

Quantum hardware platforms, including superconducting qubits and trapped ions, continue to advance. Quantum coherence and error correction are essential considerations in hardware development. Quantum hardware is increasingly accessible to researchers and developers, opening the door to practical QML applications.

14.4.2 Quantum Software

Quantum software development is crucial for implementing quantum algorithms and applications. Quantum development frameworks and libraries, such as Qiskit and Cirq, enable the programming of quantum circuits. Hybrid quantum-classical computing models are used to address practical QML challenges.

14.4.3 Real-World Applications

Quantum Machine Learning has promising applications in various industries. In finance, QML can optimize portfolio management. In healthcare, it can aid drug discovery and disease diagnosis. In materials science, QML can accelerate materials discovery. Case studies illustrate the potential of QML for solving complex problems and achieving quantum advantage.

14.5 Challenges and Future Directions

14.5.1 Quantum Advantage

Quantum advantage occurs when quantum computers outperform classical computers in specific problems. Demonstrations of quantum advantage have already been seen in applications like factoring large numbers and simulating quantum systems. The identification of additional quantum advantage scenarios is an ongoing pursuit.

14.5.2 Quantum-Safe Machine Learning

As quantum computers advance, the need for quantum-safe machine learning becomes critical. Quantum-resistant cryptography and quantum-safe algorithms are necessary to protect sensitive data and ensure long-term security in a post-quantum era.

14.5.3 Open Problems and Research Directions

Quantum Machine Learning presents many open problems and research directions. These include quantum data encoding, quantum feature selection, hybrid quantum-classical models, and quantum error correction. Addressing these challenges will be vital to harnessing the full potential of QML.

14.6 state-of-the-art quantum machine learning models

1. Quantum Support Vector Machine (QSVM): QSVM is a quantum algorithm for classification tasks. It leverages quantum interference to enhance classification accuracy and has applications in various fields.

2. Quantum Variational Algorithms: These algorithms use parameterized quantum circuits (PQCs) to approximate solutions to optimization problems. Notable examples include the Quantum Approximate Optimization Algorithm (QAOA) for combinatorial optimization.

3. Quantum Neural Networks (QNN): QNNs are quantum analogs of classical neural networks. Quantum gates serve as activation functions, enabling quantum parallelism in deep learning tasks.

Please note that the field of quantum machine learning is rapidly evolving, and new models and algorithms are continuously being developed. For the latest advancements, consider referring to research papers and updates from the quantum computing and quantum machine learning communities.

14.7 Implementation

Implementing quantum machine learning models typically requires access to quantum hardware or simulators. However, I can provide you with a Python code snippet that demonstrates the use of the Qiskit library to run a simple quantum circuit. While this is a basic quantum circuit, it serves as a starting point for more complex quantum machine learning implementations.

First, make sure you have Qiskit installed. You can install it using pip:

!pip install qiskit

Here's an example code that creates and runs a simple quantum circuit using Qiskit:

```
import numpy as np
from qiskit import QuantumCircuit, transpile, assemble, Aer, execute
from qiskit.visualization import plot_histogram
# Create a quantum circuit with 2 qubits and 2 classical bits
circuit = QuantumCircuit(2, 2)
# Apply Hadamard gates to both qubits
circuit.h(0)
circuit.h(1)
# Measure the qubits and map the results to the classical bits
circuit.measure(0, 0)
circuit.measure(1, 1)

# Simulate the quantum circuit on a local simulator
simulator = Aer.get_backend('qasm_simulator')
compiled_circuit = transpile(circuit, simulator)
job = execute(compiled_circuit, simulator, shots=1024)
result = job.result()

# Get and display the measurement results
counts = result.get_counts()
print(counts)
plot_histogram(counts)
```

This code creates a quantum circuit with two qubits, applies Hadamard gates, measures the qubits, and simulates the circuit on a local quantum simulator. The measurement results are then displayed as a histogram.

Keep in mind that this is a basic quantum circuit and doesn't directly implement a machine learning model. To use quantum machine learning models like QSVM or QAOA, you would need to follow specific algorithms and adapt them to your problem.

For more advanced quantum machine learning tasks, consider using Qiskit's quantum machine learning libraries or other quantum computing platforms. Additionally, you may need to have access to quantum hardware for real-world applications.

Quantum Neural Networks (QNNs) are a fascinating area of quantum machine learning, where quantum gates are used as activation functions within a neural network. To implement a simple Quantum Neural Network using Qiskit, you can follow this example. In this example, we'll create a simple QNN with a single quantum layer, and we'll use a quantum circuit to perform the activation function.

pip install qiskit

Here's a Python code snippet for a basic Quantum Neural Network:

```python
import numpy as np
from qiskit import QuantumCircuit, transpile, assemble, Aer, execute
from qiskit.visualization import plot_histogram
# Create a quantum circuit with 1 qubit and 1 classical bit
circuit = QuantumCircuit(1, 1)
# Define a parameter for the quantum gate (you can optimize this parameter)
theta = np.pi / 2  # Example parameter


# Apply a quantum gate with a parameter as the activation function
circuit.ry(theta, 0)
# Measure the qubit and map the result to the classical bit
circuit.measure(0, 0)
# Simulate the quantum circuit on a local simulator
simulator = Aer.get_backend('qasm_simulator')
compiled_circuit = transpile(circuit, simulator)
job = execute(compiled_circuit, simulator, shots=1024)
result = job.result()
# Get and display the measurement results
counts = result.get_counts()
print(counts)
plot_histogram(counts)
```

In this code, we create a quantum circuit with one qubit, apply a quantum gate with a parameter (the "theta" angle in this case), and measure the qubit. The parameter can be optimized during training to perform various transformations.

Keep in mind that this is a basic example. In a real Quantum Neural Network, you'd have multiple layers, a more complex architecture, and training procedures that adapt the quantum gate parameters to minimize a loss function.

Qiskit provides tools for creating more advanced QNNs, and you can explore more complex circuits and quantum activation functions as your understanding of quantum machine learning deepens.

Exercise Chapter 14:

Multiple Choice

1. What is the difference between quantum machine learning and classical machine learning?

    o A. Quantum machine learning uses quantum computers to train and deploy machine learning models.

    o B. Quantum machine learning uses quantum algorithms to solve machine learning problems.

    o C. Quantum machine learning can solve machine learning problems that are intractable for classical machine learning algorithms.

    o D. All of the above.

2. What are some of the potential applications of quantum machine learning?

    o A. Drug discovery

    o B. Material science

    o C. Financial modeling

    o D. All of the above

3. What are some of the challenges of quantum machine learning?

    o A. Quantum computers are still in their early stages of development.

    o B. Quantum machine learning algorithms can be complex and difficult to implement.

    o C. Quantum machine learning models can be sensitive to noise and errors.

    o D. All of the above

True/False

1. Quantum machine learning algorithms can be used to solve any type of machine learning problem. (False)

2. Quantum machine learning models are always more accurate than classical machine learning models. (False)

3. Quantum machine learning is a relatively new field of research, and there is still much to learn. (True)

4. Quantum machine learning has the potential to revolutionize many industries. (True)

Short Answer

1. What are some of the different types of quantum machine learning algorithms?

2. Explain how quantum machine learning can be used to accelerate the training of a classical machine learning model.

3. What are some of the ways to improve the robustness of quantum machine learning models to noise and errors?

4. Describe the process of evaluating the performance of a quantum machine learning model.

Long Answer

1. Write a blog post about the basics of quantum machine learning and its potential applications.

2. Implement a simple quantum machine learning algorithm, such as the Deutsch-Jozsa algorithm, to solve a classic machine learning problem.

3. Compare the performance of a quantum machine learning algorithm to a classical machine learning algorithm on a specific task.

4. Write a research paper on the use of quantum machine learning in a specific domain, such as drug discovery or financial modeling.